DEATH & RESURRECTION

Death & Resurrection

The Shape and Function of a Literary Motif in the Book of Acts

DENNIS J. HORTON

◆PICKWICK *Publications* • Eugene, Oregon

DEATH AND RESURRECTION
The Shape and Function of a Literary Motif in the Book of Acts

Copyright © 2009 Dennis J. Horton. All rights reserved. Except for brief quotations in critical publications or reviews, no part of this book may be reproduced in any manner without prior written permission from the publisher. Write: Permissions, Wipf and Stock Publishers, 199 W. 8th Ave., Suite 3, Eugene, OR 97401.

Scripture quotations are from the New Revised Standard Version Bible, copyright © 1989 National Council of the Churches of Christ in the United States of America. Used by permission. All rights reserved.

Pickwick Publications
A Division of Wipf and Stock Publishers
199 W. 8th Ave., Suite 3
Eugene, OR 97401

www.wipfandstock.com

ISBN 13: 978-1-60608-290-4

Cataloging-in-Publication data:

Horton, Dennis J.

Death and resurrection : the shape and function of a literary motif in the book of Acts / Dennis J. Horton

    xvi + 136 p. ; 23 cm. Includes bibliographical references and indexes.

    ISBN 13: 978-1-60608-290-4

    1. Bible. N.T. Acts—Criticism, interpretation, etc. 2. Death—Biblical teaching. 3. Resurrection—Biblical teaching. I. Title.

BS2625.6.D5 H67 2009

Manufactured in the U.S.A.

*In appreciation to Mikeal C. Parsons,
and to my wife, Sara, and son, Joel*

Contents

Abbreviations ix

Foreword xiii

Preface xv

Introduction 1

1 Diegesis and the Messianic Model: "Telling" the Motif 13

2 Mimesis and the Major Characters: "Showing" the Motif (Part I) 39

3 Mimesis and the Minor Characters: "Showing" the Motif (Part II) 61

4 Intensification through Contrast: The Secondary Motif of Death and Decay 79

Conclusion 103

Bibliography 113

Index of Modern Authors 125

Index of Scripture and Ancient Writings 128

Abbreviations

Abbreviations of biblical books, ancient texts, periodicals, and reference works used in the contents of this study are derived from the lists in *The SBL Handbook of Style* (Peabody, MA: Hendrickson, 1999) and *The Chicago Manual of Style*, 15th ed. (Chicago: University of Chicago Press, 2003). With the exception of single words and phrases, which are translated by the author, all English quotations from the New Testament, Old Testament, and Apocrypha are from the New Revised Standard Version, unless noted otherwise. Frequently cited works and those of particular relevance to this study are abbreviated as follows:

AB	Anchor Bible
AnBib	Analecta biblica
ANTC	Abingdon New Testament Commentaries
Ant.	Josephus *Antiquities of the Jews*
AR	*Archiv für Religionswissenschaft*
ATR	*Anglican Theological Review*
BAR	*Biblical Archaeology Review*
BDAG	Bauer, W., F. W. Danker, W. F. Arndt, and F. W. Gingrich, *Greek-English Lexicon of the New Testament and Other Early Christian Literature*. 3rd ed. Chicago, 2000
BDB	Brown, F., S. R. Driver, and C. A. Briggs, *A Hebrew and English Lexicon of the Old Testament*. Oxford, 1907
BECNT	Baker Exegetical Commentary of the New Testament
BETL	Bibliotheca ephemeridum theologicarum lovaniensium
BTB	*Biblical Theology Bulletin*
BWANT	Beiträge zur Wissenschaft vom Alten und Neuen Testament

Abbreviations

BZNW	Beihefte zur Zeitschrift für die neutestamentliche Wissenschaft
CBQ	Catholic Biblical Quarterly
ChrLit	Christianity and Literature
CTQ	Concordia Theological Quarterly
ETL	Ephemerides theologicae lovanienses
ExpTim	Expository Times
FF	Foundations and Facets
GBS	Guides to Biblical Scholarship
GNS	Good News Studies
HDR	Harvard Dissertations in Religion
HTR	Harvard Theological Review
HvTSt	Hervormde teologiese studies
ICC	International Critical Commentary
Int	Interpretation
JBL	Journal of Biblical Literature
JETS	Journal of the Evangelical Theological Society
JSNT	Journal for the Study of the New Testament
JSNTSup	Journal for the Study of the New Testament: Supplement Series
JSOT	Journal for the Study of the Old Testament
L.A.E.	Life of Adam and Eve
L&N	Greek-English Lexicon of the New Testament: Based on Semantic Domains. Edited by J. P. Louw and E. A. Nida. 2nd ed. New York, 1989
LCL	Loeb Classical Library
LEC	Library of Early Christianity
LXX	Septuagint
NAC	New American Commentary
NASB	New American Standard Bible
Neot	Neotestamentica
NIBCNT	New International Biblical Commentary on the New Testament
NICNT	New International Commentary on the New Testament
NovT	Novum Testamentum
NovTSup	Supplements to Novum Testamentum
NTS	New Testament Studies
NTTS	New Testament Tools and Studies

OBT	Overtures to Biblical Theology
PRSt	*Perspectives in Religious Studies*
RevExp	*Review and Expositor*
RTP	*Revue de théologie et de philosophie*
SBLCP	Society of Biblical Literature Centennial Publications
SBLDS	Society of Biblical Literature Dissertation Series
SBLMS	Society of Biblical Literature Monograph Series
SBLSP	*Society of Biblical Literature Seminar Papers*
SBT	Studies in Biblical Theology
ScEs	*Science et esprit*
SNTSMS	Society for New Testament Studies Monograph Series
SP	Sacra pagina
StZ	*Stimmen der Zeit*
TLG	Berkowitz and Squitier, *Thesaurus linguae graecae: Canon of Greek Authors and Works*.
TNTC	Tyndale New Testament Commentaries
TynBul	*Tyndale Bulletin*
VT	*Vetus Testamentum*
VTSup	Supplements to Vetus Testamentum
War	Josephus *Wars of the Jews*
WBC	Word Biblical Commentary
WC	Westminster Commentaries
WUNT	Wissenschaftliche Untersuchungen zum Neuen Testament
ZAW	*Zeitschrift für die alttestamentliche Wissenschaft*
ZNW	*Zeitschrift für die neutestamentliche Wissenschaft und die Kunde derälteren Kirche*

Foreword

For far too long, the Lukan writings have been viewed as an unwanted "step-child," when considered alongside the "theological genius" of Paul or the author of the Fourth Gospel. In particular, Luke has been criticized for advocating a triumphalistic "theology of glory" that pales when compared with Paul's more theologically astute "theology of the cross." Reactions to this oversimplified and somewhat entrenched view that have emphasized the church's suffering in Acts (to the neglect of the resurrection) are likewise inadequate. Either reading is, in my opinion, a poor misreading of the text. Finally, Dennis Horton has come along to offer a balanced assessment of Luke's theology in this regard, demonstrating that death *and* resurrection are inextricably tied together as a central literary motif in the Lukan narrative of Acts. The study continues to be relevant today to those Christian communities seeking a word of hope and life in a world of suffering and death.

Although there have been a few studies on related themes, no one has addressed the issue in the same way as Horton; that is to say, no one has presented an argument that accounts for the evidence as comprehensively and competently as he does. In addition to his contributions to the exegesis of Acts, Dr. Horton also contributes greatly to our understanding of the concept of a "literary motif" (a much used and little understood term) and its potential use to describe literary features of biblical narrative. Horton's work in this area, too, stands out among those who have attempted to trace literary motifs in biblical literature for its precision and care. All in all, this is a well-argued monograph that is clear and concise and deserves a careful hearing by those interested in the death and resurrection motif in Acts, in particular, and in theological and literary readings of Acts, in general.

Mikeal Parsons, Professor and Macon Chair in Religion
Baylor University

Preface

This work, originally a doctoral dissertation presented to the graduate faculty of Baylor University's Department of Religion in 1995, examines the motif of death and resurrection in Acts. The shape and function of the motif become clear by applying William Freedman's criteria of a literary motif to the Acts narrative. The methodology for this study follows a threefold procedure: (1) an examination of the diegetic references to death and resurrection; (2) an analysis of mimetic examples of this messianic pattern among the experiences of major and minor characters; and (3) a demonstration of the way the motif becomes intensified through contrast with a secondary motif, that of death and decay. Each section includes explanations about its relevance to the identification and efficacy of the primary motif.

Through such an approach, several significant contributions become apparent. The study provides a clear example of a biblical motif and how it develops and functions within the narrative, serving as a valuable guide for future studies of biblical motifs. The work also supplies a needed balance between the extremes of past and present Lukan scholarship by considering the combined effect of suffering and renewed life within a single motif. Both the diegetic remarks and the actions of the characters reveal the importance of the two elements for Lukan theology and soteriology. The function of the motif derives from its usage within the narrative and proves insightful for gaining a better understanding of the aesthetic quality of the story while simultaneously showing how the narrator skillfully wields the motif to provide encouragement to the followers of "The Way," issue a warning to would-be persecutors, and deliver an evangelistic message to potential converts such as the "God-fearers." The messianic pattern therefore becomes a heuristic tool, which the narrator carefully plies to create a potent motif with a multifaceted message for a growing and often suffering Christian community.

It is with deep appreciation that I acknowledge the faithful support of the many people who made this work possible. First and foremost, I want to express appreciation to my wife Sara and son Joel who have patiently supported me during the revision and editing process of this work. Second, I wish to acknowledge the continual inspiration and guidance of Mikeal Parsons, mentor and friend. Several other scholars have also been personally helpful. In particular, Alan Culpepper and David Moessner provided substantive critiques and guidance in the development of the original material for the dissertation. The works of such scholars as Robert Tannehill, Richard Pervo, Robert Funk, William Freedman, and many others have further informed my thinking and contributed to the development of the thesis. Besides these, Naymond Keathley and James Kennedy contributed valuable guidance at the project's inception and served admirably during the completion phase of the original work. I am also grateful to my Ministry Guidance colleague, Jeter Basden, and my administrative associate, Louine Adams, for their support and encouragement. Finally, I wish to thank Chris Spinks and the editorial staff of Wipf and Stock Publishers and my graduate assistant, Courtney Lyons, for their assistance with the formatting and editing of the material in preparation for its publication.

Introduction

With the advent of narrative criticism into the field of biblical studies, the examination of literary "motifs" currently enjoys vigorous attention.[1] In the last two decades, students have produced over seventy dissertations that relate directly to this literary device and its application to biblical texts.[2] Yet among these works, many of the writers fail to provide an adequate definition of "motif," sometimes providing a simple, generic definition or no definition at all. The result is the same in both cases: "motif" as a literary technique becomes diluted, easily replaced with such words as "theme," "concept," or "topic."[3]

A generic understanding of the literary motif naturally leads to an abundant number of sightings in the biblical texts, attributing less significance to each case. Current usage of the term qualifies nearly anything as a motif. William Freedman criticizes the zeal of those readers who seem to "find a motif in every cupboard,"[4] or in our case, every biblical text. Proliferation of the generic view of motif necessarily entails a loss of specificity, consequently diminishing the value of motif as an analytical tool. Without clarity of definition, motif is as helpful to the biblical scholar as bifocals are to a surgeon performing microscopic surgery.

    1. "Motif" here refers to the broad inclusive sense. A more specialized meaning, as the term will function in this work, will be defined in the following pages.

    2. Some of those that focus on a literary motif in Acts include Kim, "'From Israel to the Nations'"; Aubert, "Shepherd-Flock Motif"; Elledge, "Resurrection and the End of History"; and Frein, "Literary Significance of the Jesus-as-Prophet Motif."

    3. See Harvey, "The 'With Christ' Motif" as an example of this problem. His article begins: "Although Paul uses the 'with Christ' *motif* 36 times in his letters, few extended treatments of the *theme* have been attempted . . . When the 'with Christ' *concept* . . ." (329; italics added). Harvey could have just as easily substituted "phrase" for "motif" and actually does so later in the same paragraph.

    4. Freedman, "Literary Motif," 127.

DEATH AND RESURRECTION

PURPOSE AND DEFINITIONS

Utilizing Freedman's criteria for identifying and describing an efficacious motif reduces the blurred understanding of this literary tool, thereby preventing undesirable consequences for biblical scholarship. Freedman delineates five specific qualifications for an effective motif: (1) frequency, (2) avoidability, (3) occurrence in significant contexts, (4) coherency, and (5) symbolic appropriateness.[5] The better the motif satisfies these criteria, the more effective and beneficial the analysis. Freedman also provides a necessarily lengthy definition in accordance with his criteria:

> A motif, then, is a recurrent theme, character, or verbal pattern, but it may also be a family or associational cluster of literal or figurative references to a given class of concepts or objects, whether it be animals, machines, circles, music, or whatever. It is generally symbolic—that is, it can be seen to carry a meaning beyond the literal one immediately apparent; it represents on the verbal level something characteristic of the structure of the work, the events, the characters, the emotional effects or the moral or cognitive content. It is presented both as an object of description and, more often, as part of the narrator's imagery and descriptive vocabulary. And it indispensably requires a certain minimal frequency of recurrence and improbability of appearance in order both to make itself at least subconsciously felt and to indicate its purposiveness.[6]

This work then will seek to apply Freedman's specifications to the unified concept of death and resurrection in the book of Acts.

Although originally intended for the study of modern literature, Freedman's motif criteria prove equally insightful for evaluation of the Acts narrative. Both the contemporary novel and its ancient counterparts share many of the same traits, including the presence of strong themes, symbolism, characters, plots, contrasts, etc. For this reason, biblical scholars have spawned a plethora of works in which they apply modern narrative theory to ancient texts.[7] The ancient author's awareness of narrative techniques in story may be indeterminable. We can, however, identify the

---

5. Ibid., 126–27.
6. Ibid., 127–28.
7. David Rhoads and Donald Michie in their work on the Gospel of Mark (*Mark as Story*) and R. Alan Culpepper's analysis of John (*Anatomy of the Fourth Gospel*) became the major forerunners of many other studies that apply modern narrative theory to the biblical texts.

presence or absence of a particular technique (such as the use of a motif) within the text. This work will not seek to prove authorial intention but rather will identify the possible presence of a death-resurrection motif as defined according to modern criteria and, if present, determine its specific shape and function within the Acts narrative.[8]

In the past, scholars have tended to downplay the role of Jesus's suffering and death in Luke-Acts, attributing greater importance to the resurrection event. When compared to Paul's writings, both C. H. Dodd and J. M. Creed found that the speeches in Acts present a theologically barren view of the cross. For this reason, they concluded that Luke's writings, in contrast to the Pauline interpretation of Jesus's death, lack a developed "theology of the cross"—*theologia crucis*.[9] Instead, Luke was understood to attribute greatest value to the elements of Jesus's glory through his resurrection and ascension. Ernst Käsemann provided the apex of this school of thought in 1964 when he proclaimed that in Acts, "a *theologia gloriae* is now in process of replacing the *theologia crucis*."[10] Though not stated as dramatically, I. Howard Marshall affirmed the position that in Acts, Jesus's resurrection supersedes the importance of his death.[11] Joseph Tyson, in his thorough study of Jesus's death in Luke-Acts, continues to accent a Lukan theology of glory especially in terms of soteriological significance. He concludes, "The benefits of forgiveness of sins and the Spirit are more closely connected with the resurrection [of Jesus] than the death."[12] Similarly, Joel B. Green attributes greater significance to Jesus's resurrection, judging it to be the "central affirmation of the Christian message in the Acts of the Apostles."[13] As such, the resurrection of Jesus is the key event for Lukan Christology and soteriology, being both the "means and nature of salvation."[14]

An emphasis on the Lukan theology of glory persists through the present. One of the most comprehensive recent works is Kevin L. Anderson's treatise on Jesus's resurrection in Luke-Acts, "But God Raised

8. The hyphenated term "death-resurrection" will serve to emphasize the unified nature of the motif.
9. Dodd, *Apostolic Preaching*, 25; Creed, *Gospel according to St. Luke*, lxxii.
10. Käsemann, *Essays on New Testament Themes*, 92.
11. Marshall, "Resurrection in the Acts," 92–107.
12. Tyson, *Death of Jesus in Luke-Acts*, 170.
13. Green, "'Witnesses of His Resurrection,'" 227.
14. Ibid., 237.

Him from the Dead." Anderson contends that the resurrection is the pivotal event in Luke's narrative in all respects: theologically, christologically, ecclesiologically, and eschatologically.[15] All of these different aspects of resurrection relate to the Lukan message of salvation.[16] Though Anderson acknowledges the importance of other events in Luke-Acts such as Jesus's ministry, death, and outpouring of the Spirit, he clearly locates the "focus" of soteriology within the resurrection event.[17] Jesus's suffering and death do not convey forgiveness of sins; rather, only the resurrection, God's reversal of that death, "has a lasting salvific effect."[18]

Some biblical scholarship, however, has countered this perceived dominance of a Lukan theology of glory by positing a strong emphasis on Jesus's suffering and death in Luke-Acts. Georg Braumann in 1963 became one of the first dissenting voices, arguing that the theology of Luke is primarily a *theologia crucis*.[19] More recently, David Moessner has revealed many of the shortcomings inherent with the triumphalistic approach to understanding Luke-Acts. Moreover, his appreciation for the effects of Jesus's rejection and death significantly expands the theological role of suffering in Luke's writings.[20] As a result, Moessner's well-argued thesis has attracted scholarly support and prompted further studies on the topic. Both Robert Tannehill and John Polhill, for example, reflect an indebtedness to Moessner's position.[21] Paul R. House identifies suffering as the most essential element of Acts.[22] Charles Estridge likewise emphasizes the importance of suffering by highlighting its centrality to

---

15. Anderson, *"But God Raised Him"*, 13.

16. Ibid.

17. Ibid., 31.

18. Ibid., 41. Anderson further clarifies: "Each of these events is crucial to salvation history, but the resurrection of Jesus stands as the focal point in the salvation message" (41).

19. Braumann, "Mittel der Zeit," 121. See also Schütz, who develops Braumann's thesis in the 1969 publication of his *Der leidende Christus*, explaining the theological significance of the close connection between Jesus's suffering and that of his followers.

20. Moessner has written several pieces about this topic, but two of special interest include "'Christ Must Suffer': New Light" and "'Christ Must Suffer,' the Church Must Suffer," abbreviated hereafter as "New Light" and "Church," respectively.

21. Tannehill, *Narrative Unity of Luke-Acts*, 2:114, 182, 348; Polhill, *Acts*, 70, 319.

22. House, "Suffering and the Purpose of Luke-Acts," 317–30. House states emphatically: "In short, Acts has no purpose, no plot, no structure, and no history without suffering" (321).

the speeches in Acts.[23] More recently, Scott Cunningham has expounded on the theology of persecution as a theme in Luke-Acts, highlighting its importance and functions.[24] Others, such as Martin Mittelstadt, have followed Cunningham's lead with special emphasis in Acts on suffering and its implications for the community of believers.[25]

Even as a number of biblical scholars are embracing a *theologia crucis* as the most appropriate lens for envisioning Lukan soteriology and ecclesiology, the positive focus on redemptive suffering has its detractors. Many contextual theologians (feminists, womanists, and those representing racially oppressed groups) express strong reservations about attributing the greatest value to Jesus's passion, especially when his suffering is viewed in isolation from his life and the vindication of his death through resurrection.[26] They reason that a strong emphasis on crucifixion theology sanctions violence and fosters victimization.[27] Admittedly, contextual theologians often read against the grain of individual biblical texts, making many of their claims beyond the purview of the present study.[28] Nevertheless, a more balanced approach that values both Jesus's suffering and resurrection as a unified concept does serve to ameliorate some of the suspected problems associated with a disproportionate emphasis on crucifixion theology.

23. Estridge, "Suffering in Contexts."

24. Cunningham, *"Through Many Tribulations."* Cunningham's exhaustive treatment of Jesus's suffering and death serves as a fitting counterpoint to Anderson's comprehensive study on Jesus's resurrection. Their well-supported, but opposing emphases provide added impetus for serious consideration of a single motif inclusive of both Jesus's death and resurrection.

25. Mittelstadt, *Spirit and Suffering*, esp. 12–20.

26. Patterson, *Beyond the Passion*, 3–4. Patterson understands that nearly all of the biblical statements about Jesus's death were "calculated to resurrect the significance of Jesus' life for those who loved him, and would come to love him in the years ahead. They spoke of the movement he began as 'the way'—his way of life" (4).

27. See Brock and Parker, *Proverbs of Ashes*; Weaver, *Nonviolent Atonement*; and Terrell, *Power in the Blood?* Though negative ramifications may be associated with a soteriology restricted to crucifixion theology, other scholars provide considered responses that retain the salvific value of the cross without sanctioning violence (cf. Thompson, *Crossing the Divide*; and Talbert's discussion of the topic in his Smyth & Helwys commentary on *Romans* (140–44).

28. The present study treats the text as primary for developing a biblical theology, whereas contextual theologians have various means of developing their theological tenets, often using the biblical texts as secondary support or to establish general principles that can be applied in different contexts.

Some scholars do support the concept that both the death and resurrection/ascension of Jesus receive equal emphasis in Luke-Acts. While C. K. Barrett acknowledges Luke's portrayal of an unhindered gospel, he also notes that the followers of Jesus who carry this gospel travel by the "way of the cross."[29] Nevertheless, Barrett does not perceive a fully developed theology of either stripe in the Lukan writings.

> It would perhaps be wrong to describe him [Luke] as either a theologus gloriae or a theologus crucis: he is not sufficiently interested in theology (beyond basic Christian convictions) to be called a theologus of any colour. But he knows that to be a Christian is to take up a cross daily, and what this meant in the first century he has described in vivid narrative. This strictly practical theologia crucis is not contradicted by the fact that his pilgrims can "shout as they travel the wilderness through." [30]

Beverly Roberts Gaventa, attributing greater theological depth to Luke-Acts, appropriately perceives a balanced *and vital* role for both theological perspectives: "Both of these threads, the triumph of God who will not allow the gospel to be overcome *and* the rejection of the gospel and the persecution of its apostles, belong to the narrative Luke develops. To eliminate either of them is to miss something essential to the Lukan story."[31] Additionally, Morna Hooker finds soteriological value associated with both events in Luke's writings: "forgiveness of sins . . . is now available for all—through his death *and resurrection*."[32]

Consideration of the evidence utilizing motif analysis confirms equal importance of these two connected events in the Acts narrative. Through the combination of speeches (inclusive of the narrator's comments) and actions of the characters, Luke forges the elements of death and resurrection into a solitary motif. Cunningham acknowledges the equal value of both elements, but he mistakenly separates the two.[33] The present study

---

29. Barrett, "Theologia Crucis—in Acts?," 79.
30. Ibid., 84.
31. Gaventa, "Towards a Theology of Acts," 157.
32. Hooker, *Not Ashamed of the Gospel*, 91.
33. Cunningham, *"Through Many Tribulations"*, 324. Cunningham states, "In fact, the theology of glory and the theology of the cross are both equally affirmed by the narrative." His study, however, focuses exclusively on the suffering/persecution perspective. As a result, he fails to integrate the two elements as they are within the Luke-Acts narrative. Nevertheless, his work does provide a thorough explication of Luke's theology of the

proposes a double-edged yet single literary motif formed by diegetic references to Jesus's death and resurrection. Many of the characters in Acts reinforce this motif through their own experiences as portrayed through several different mimetic scenes. Finally, the juxtaposition of the contrasting death-and-decay motif heightens the effects of the primary motif.

The following definitions will help clarify some of the narrative terminology necessary for accomplishing the goals of this study. "Diegesis," as Robert W. Funk defines, is the classical term that refers to the "recounting" or "telling" of events in the "unfocused or mediated narrative segment."[34] Many of the summary statements, for example, fall into this category and may be termed "hyperdiegetic" statements because the narrator stands "at the first level above the primary narrative."[35] Because the speeches in Acts are embedded within the first level of the narrative, the speaker becomes the narrator within the story. Events recounted on this deeper level will therefore be termed "intradiegetic."[36]

"Mimesis," then, refers to the "enacting" or "showing" of events in the focused scene; that is, a scene in which "the narrator transports the listener or reader, by means of words, to a specific time and place, with participants present and allows her or him to look on and listen in."[37] In contrast to the unfocused segment, the mimetic scene utilizes specific language appealing to the senses, particularly to sight and hearing. As such, mimesis functions well to describe the experiences of the characters in Acts.

Freedman, as explained above, furnishes valuable clarification for a comprehensive understanding of motif as a literary technique. He emphasizes that a motif "may appear as something described" in the narrative, but "perhaps even more often forms part of the description. It slips, as it were, into the author's vocabulary, into the dialogue, and into his [sic] imagery . . . ."[38] In a related article, Freedman offers a concrete example of this phenomenon: the motif of circularity in Theodore Dreiser's *Sister*

---

cross in Acts and its implications those who become followers of Jesus.

34. Funk, *Poetics of Biblical Narrative*, 134.

35. Ibid., 154.

36. Ibid., 31–33, 154. Though the meanings of such terms may be nuanced slightly by different authors, Funk's particular definitions are well-suited for the present task and comport well with contemporary opinion of the guild.

37. Ibid., 134–35.

38. Freedman, "Literary Motif," 124–25.

8   DEATH AND RESURRECTION

Carrie. Not only does the narrator recount instances of circularity, the movement of the main character "is a repetitive, futile, in effect circular quest for happiness."[39] Because the narrator of Acts, as in *Sister Carrie*, both "tells" (diegesis) and "shows" (mimesis) the message, the application of Funk's distinctions between these two types of narration in conjunction with Freedman's criteria adeptly identifies and gauges the effectiveness of the death-resurrection motif in Acts.

BACKGROUND

I first became intrigued with the topic of this study while reading Richard Pervo's *Luke's Story of Paul*. By analyzing the imagery used to describe Peter's final imprisonment (Acts 12) and Paul's shipwreck (Acts 27), Pervo suggests that Luke's depictions of these events create a symbolic death-resurrection experience for each character.[40] As part of my graduate course work, I explored the theological implications of symbolic death and resurrection in Acts among the major and minor characters. Further consideration of this phenomenon within a literary motif, as well as discussions with Baylor colleagues, raised the prospect about Luke's use of this double-sided narrative device as a central role in the Acts narrative. I then presented some preliminary findings in a paper at a regional meeting for the Society of Biblical Literature.

My research in the area has revealed a need for explication of the proposed motif. On the diegetic level, as noted earlier, scholars have preferred to tip the hermeneutical scales in one direction (glory) or the other (suffering) rather than exploring the ramifications of an equally balanced double-sided motif. Richard Rackham, M. D. Goulder, Walter Radl, Richard Pervo, and Susan Garrett have conducted preliminary research on the mimetic concept of symbolic death and resurrection, but this research either lacks substantiation or neglects the role of the minor characters.[41] Scholarly research has assessed the actions of certain minor characters within Acts, but no research has related these characters with the unifying motif of death and resurrection.[42]

    39. Freedman, "A Look at Dreiser," 386.
    40. Pervo, *Luke's Story of Paul*, 44, 92–93.
    41. Rackham, *Acts* (1904); Goulder, *Type and History in Acts* (1964); Radl, *Paulus und Jesus* (1975); Pervo, *Luke's Story of Paul* (1990); and Garrett, "Exodus from Bondage" (1990).
    42. M. Dennis Hamm explores both the symbolic implications of the healing of the

METHODOLOGY

To determine the shape and function of the death-resurrection motif, I will apply Freedman's criteria to the Acts narrative using a threefold procedure: (1) examine the diegetic references to death and resurrection; (2) isolate mimetic examples of the death-resurrection pattern among the experiences of major and minor characters; and (3) demonstrate how the motif becomes intensified through contrast with a secondary motif of death and decay. Each section will include explanations about its relevance to the identification and efficacy of the primary motif.

Chapter 1 will consider the diegetic statements in Acts about death and resurrection. This section will examine how these references emphasize Jesus's passion and resurrection as an inseparable climactic event, frequently recounted in the teaching and preaching of the early church. Particular attention will be given to the placement of these references, possible interpretations, and significance for the development of the motif.

Because the message is both told and shown, the second and third chapters examine the death-resurrection experiences of the major and minor characters. Parallelism and symbolism with insights from reader response criticism provide the primary means of validation for such occurrences. The parallels consist of pertinent similarities in vocabulary, phrases, activity, and sequence found within Acts, and between Acts and the Third Gospel.[43] The symbols for death and resurrected life encompass ancestral and cultural symbols as well as those created by the implied

---

temple beggar ("Acts 3:12–26," 199–217) and the healing of Paul ("Paul's Blindness," 63–72), Robert O'Toole discusses some of the symbolic overtones of ἀνίστημι ("Some Observations on *Anistēmi*," 85–92), and Bernard Trémel offers a symbolic interpretation of the Eutychus episode ("À propos d'Actes 20,7–12," 359–69).

43. The study of parallelism in Luke and Acts has produced a rich history, including works by F. C. Baur, Hans Conzelmann, Charles H. Talbert, and more recently Robert F. O'Toole and David P. Moessner. Although these studies focus primarily on theological or pastoral concerns and have neglected the minor characters, many of their insights prove informative for the present study.

author.⁴⁴ The final criterion utilizes reader expectations and retrospection to help clarify the meaning of the texts.⁴⁵

In addition to these three means of control, other complementary measures will verify the distinctiveness of the death-resurrection scenes. The immediate context will, in some cases, provide interpretive clues for confirmation of the pattern.⁴⁶ Obviously not all healings, imprisonments, or shipwrecks in ancient Mediterranean literature indicate the presence of a death-resurrection experience.⁴⁷ The accompanying explanations within these chapters will therefore focus attention on those factors that validate the presence of substantive allusions to the messianic pattern.

The fourth chapter will set forth a contrasting death-and-decay motif. The same procedure of examining diegetic segments and mimetic scenes will document the extent of the motif in juxtaposition with the death-resurrection motif. Descriptions of the secondary motif will highlight its effects on and relation to the primary motif.

The conclusion will synthesize the findings of the study, clarifying the shape and function of the motif within the narrative. This section will also suggest ways in which the message of the motif relates to other emphases in Acts and to other areas of biblical research and ancient Greco-Roman study.

---

44. Mark Allan Powell provides clarification: "*Symbols of ancestral vitality* derive their meaning from earlier sources. . . . *Symbols of cultural range* derive their meaning from the social and historical context of the real author and his or her community. . . . *Symbols created by the implied author* can be understood only with the context of the particular narrative" (*What Is Narrative Criticism?* 29).

45. Of particular importance are the works by Robert Alter, Janice Capel Anderson, Fred Burnett, and Robert Tannehill on type-scenes and redundancy.

46. E.g., the healing of the lame beggar at the temple receives many interpretive clues from the surrounding and interwoven materials (Acts 2–4).

47. Within Acts, for instance, the healing of the spirit-possessed slave at Philippi does not reflect a movement from a state of death to one of life. In other contemporary literature, Apollonius of Tyana heals the blind and the lame but fails to initiate a death-resurrection pattern (Philostratus *Life of Appolonius*, 1:317). Xenophon of Ephesus narrates the story of two young lovers who undergo numerous imprisonments and shipwrecks, yet he conveys the theme of constant suffering in these scenes, not suffering and renewed life (Xenophon *Ephesian Tale*).

LIMITATIONS

In order to thoroughly analyze the specific shape and function of the motif within the Acts narrative, this study will necessarily focus its attention on the book of Acts. Nevertheless, this limitation does not imply the absence of the death-resurrection motif in the Third Gospel. Incipient forms of the motif do seem to be present in Luke's Gospel, and some of the experiences involving actual death and resuscitation/resurrection prove informative for the interpretation of similar events in Acts.[48] Particular attention will be given to the Third Gospel's treatment of Jesus's passion and resurrection to identify any parallels with the major and minor characters in Acts.

Despite a definite interrelationship between Luke and Acts, a complete narrative unity remains elusive and should not be assumed. Mikeal C. Parsons and Richard I. Pervo, for example, have challenged this assumption and recommend a thorough reexamination of the issue.[49] A full analysis of the motif within the Third Gospel deserves a separate study, perhaps as a sequel to the present work. Rather than forcing the two narratives into a single story, this study presents them as independent but related stories, allowing the Gospel to provide interpretive clues, not mandates, for understanding the Acts narrative.

The relationship of the motif to the entire plot of Acts, though certainly a potentially fruitful topic, also lies beyond the parameters of the present study. Preliminary evidence does reveal that the motif becomes especially prominent at climactic points of the narrative, indicating the significance of the death-resurrection message for the story. Nevertheless, to perform a thorough analysis of the plot would require in itself a detailed explanation of theory and thereby distract from the primary concern: the shape and function of the motif. Examination of plot will be limited to elementary comments relating to Freedman's third criterion for a motif, that of its occurrence in significant contexts.

---

48. E.g., the widow's son (Luke 7:11–17), Jairus's daughter (Luke 8:41–56), and Jesus himself (Luke 22:1—24:53).

49. Parsons and Pervo, *Rethinking the Unity of Luke and Acts*, 45–83.

POTENTIAL CONTRIBUTIONS

Such a study proves valuable in at least three substantive ways. First, this study provides an instructive example of a literary motif within a biblical text, clarifying how a motif can saturate the narrative and become intensified through contrast with a subordinate motif. Subsequently, a practical guide and comprehensive example exists for future research on biblical motifs.

Second, this study supplies a needed balance between the extremes of past and present scholarship by considering the combination of suffering and renewed life within a single motif. Moreover, interaction with those who accent one theological perspective over the other (*theologia gloria* or *theologia crucis*) creates an instructive dialogue, enriching the academic conversation about Lukan theology.

Third, clarification of the death-resurrection motif yields practical implications for the contemporary church. Demonstration of both suffering and renewed life as integral parts of Lukan discipleship provides a better balance for understanding the Lukan view of the Christian life. Inclusion of suffering as a common element of Christian living counters the lopsided message of those who distort the meaning of abundant life to be composed only of health, wealth, and prosperity for the faithful followers of Christ.

1

Diegesis and the Messianic Model: "Telling" the Motif

Though the Book of Acts develops multiple themes,[1] this chapter highlights the death-resurrection message presented through the diegetic remarks about Jesus. Narrator and character comments "tell" the story of Jesus, not in the focalized mimetic mode but rather in summary fashion. Not every reference to Jesus contains both elements of death and resurrection, yet numerous diegetic statements about him do consistently combine both concepts. Because some scholars have favored one perspective (either suffering or glory) over the other, this chapter engages both viewpoints.

The diegetic passages of Acts form the structure with frequent digressions to answer challenges emerging from the different interpretations. Beginning with the narrator comments on the hyperdiegetic level, the focus then shifts to the intradiegetic narrator comments, which are spoken within a deeper narrative layer by the characters themselves. In both sections, discussion begins with passages clearly including the combined death-resurrection message, followed by divergent passages with depict Jesus with only dark shades of suffering or resplendent hues of renewed life.

---

1. Polhill, *Acts*, 57–72. Polhill discusses eight different themes in his introduction, which, he claims, "all interweave and overlap with one another to furnish together the rich tapestry that is the story of Acts" (57).

HYPERDIEGETIC COMMENTS ABOUT JESUS

As mentioned previously, hyperdiegetic statements refer to those made by the narrator and that, in accordance with Robert Funk's understanding, take place on the level above the primary narrative.[2] These comments include summaries and descriptions given in "unfocused" segments where "the narrator 'reports' what has transpired without permitting the reader to witness events directly or immediately."[3] In iterative mode as used for summaries, "time, participants, actions, and even space are heaped up, pluralized, conflated."[4]

By investigating these hyperdiegetic comments, the narrator's viewpoint of Jesus takes shape. William S. Kurz gives an apt description of this perspective as "the filter through which the narrator presents his narration; it is like the place of the camera which determines the angle from which a viewer sees an object."[5] The narrator and each character or character group in a narrative express individual perspectives that may or may not be in agreement with the others. James Dawsey, for example, argues that the narrator in the Gospel of Luke has a different perspective or "voice" than the Lukan Jesus.[6] Though the academic guild has not embraced Dawsey's conclusions,[7] his work does clarify the possible distinctions between a narrator and characters within the narrative. For this reason, focusing attention on the hyperdiegetic comments contributes to a greater understanding of the narrator's view of Jesus.

This study assumes that the narrator in Acts is both reliable and authoritative; that is, the narrator merits readers' trust and guides them in a

---

2. Funk, *Poetics of Biblical Narrative*, 31. Although Gérard Genette (*Narrative Discourse*, 228) and Shlomith Rimmon-Kenan (*Narrative Fiction*, 91) both prefer the term "extradiegetic" to describe this level, I agree with Funk that this term fosters confusion and suggests that the narrator is somehow "outside" rather than part of the narrative as a whole (*Poetics*, 31 n. 16).

3. Funk, *Poetics*, 134.

4. Ibid., 139.

5. Kurz, "Narrative Approaches to Luke-Acts," 203.

6. Dawsey, *Lukan Voice*, 93–94.

7. Robert Tannehill remains unconvinced that the two voices can be distinguished so clearly from one another (*Narrative Unity of Luke-Acts*, 1:7), and Joseph B. Tyson expresses doubt that Luke's readers would be able to recognize the subtle hints left by such a narrator (review of *Lukan Voice*, 545). While making these observations, both Tannehill and Tyson offer another substantive reason for rejecting Dawsey's view—the unlikelihood of a gospel narrator's being categorized as unreliable and non-omniscient.

desired interpretation of the characters, their direct speech, and their actions.[8] Not only does the prologue itself engender readers' trust through a reassurance of the book's comprehensiveness, the easing of any doubts occurs, according to Robert Tannehill, because the "values and beliefs affirmed by the narrator are also those of the implied author."[9] In short, the narrator does not function as a foil for the implied author to convey a contradictory message.

Moreover the use of narrative asides and first-person narration legitimize and enhance the narrator's authority. Steven M. Sheeley argues convincingly that the narrative asides play a critical role by establishing a relationship in which readers learn to depend on the narrator for "much of the information necessary to read and understand the story correctly."[10] The shift from third- to first-person narration, according to Allen Walworth, augments the narrator's diegetic authority by adding the credibility of an eyewitness account.[11] The combination of techniques enables the narrator to exert influence over readers' interpretation of the story.

References to Jesus's Death and Resurrection

Two of the clearest passages in which the narrator connects death and resurrection to Jesus surface in the opening scene of the book (1:1–3) and a nutshell summary of Paul's missionary preaching (17:2–4). Besides these, the narrator alludes to Jesus as the crucified-risen Messiah in numerous abbreviated comments scattered throughout the narrative. The final part of this section investigates the possible exceptions to this dual emphasis of the narrator's understanding of Jesus.

---

8. Rimmon-Kenan defines the reliable narrator as "one whose rendering of the story and commentary on it the reader is supposed to take as an authoritative account of the fictional truth" (*Narrative Fiction*, 100). R. Alan Culpepper offers further clarification: "The reliability of the narrator . . . must be kept distinct from both the historical accuracy of the narrator's account and the 'truth' of his ideological point of view. 'Reliability' is a matter of literary analysis, historical accuracy is the territory of the historian, and 'truth' is a matter for believers and theologians" (*Anatomy of the Fourth Gospel*, 32).

9. Tannehill, *Narrative Unity*, 1:7.

10. Sheeley, "Narrative Asides," 102. He defines narrative asides here as "parenthetical remarks addressed directly to the reader which interrupt the logical progression of the story, establishing a relationship between the narrator and the narratee which exists outside the story being narrated."

11. Walworth, "Narrator of Acts," 31.

Acts 1:3

The opening words of the narrator set forth the integral components of the double-sided motif by stating that Jesus, "after his suffering . . . presented himself alive to them by many convincing proofs" (1:3). Verse three is characterized by diegesis rather than mimesis because of the iterative mode in recounting the event.[12] The narrator describes an action that occurs repeatedly over a forty day period. The mention of Jesus's "suffering" (παθεῖν) here includes his death. As Hans Conzelmann notes, the infinitive of πάσχω regularly refers to "the whole of the passion" in both Luke and Acts.[13] Now, subsequent to his death, Jesus is alive and demonstrates this with "convincing proofs." Such appearances to the apostles obviously presuppose the resurrection event. The narrator thus opens the story with a powerful image of Jesus, painting him as the one who experienced both suffering/death and resurrection.

The positioning of this portrait at the beginning of the story has a profound impact on the reader. Meir Sternberg calls such a strategy the "primacy effect," suggesting that a characterization given early in the narrative significantly influences readers' continuing perception of that character.[14] Shlomith Rimmon-Kenan concurs with Sternberg's judgment:

> The text can direct and control the reader's comprehension and attitudes by positioning *certain* items before others . . . . Thus, information and attitudes presented at an early stage of the text tend to encourage the reader to interpret everything in their light. The reader is prone to preserve such meanings and attitudes for as long as possible.[15]

The narrator's description of Jesus at this crucial point in the narrative therefore shapes all subsequent interpretations of Jesus. The narrator encourages readers to rely on this first impression of Jesus as the crucified-and-risen one whenever they encounter and judge the later images.

---

12. Funk, *Poetics*, 137–38. Relying on Genette, Funk defines "iterative" as "a technical term meaning the narration in a single statement of events occurring more than once" (137 n. 9). He later specifies three types of iterative statements: those which suggest (1) repeated action, (2) durative action, and (3) conative action (ibid., 159).

13. Conzelmann, *Acts*, 5. Cf. Luke 22:15; 24:26, 46; Acts 3:18; 17:3; 26:23.

14. Sternberg, *Expositional Modes*, 96.

15. Rimmon-Kenan, *Narrative Fiction*, 74.

Diegesis and the Messianic Model: "Telling" the Motif 17

The words spoken to the apostles about the "reign of God" (βασιλείας τοῦ θεοῦ) likely encompass both events as well. F. F. Bruce reflects this viewpoint in his commentary when he describes the reign of God in Luke as "the same good news as Jesus himself had announced earlier, but now given effective fulfillment by the saving events of his passion and triumph."[16] Jesus's words to the disciples in the Third Gospel after his resurrection further substantiate the point.[17] In contrast to the general resurrection appearances described in the opening verses of Acts, Luke 24:36–49 offers a focalized example. The narrator in Acts mentions that Jesus speaks to the apostles about the reign of God, but the closing scene of the Gospel records the actual words spoken. Here the resurrected Jesus specifically explains to them that the Messiah, as prophesied, had "to suffer and to rise from the dead on the third day" (Luke 24:46). If the correlation between the two scenes is justified, the unavoidable conclusion makes a strong connection between the reign of God and the Messiah who experiences death and resurrection. Not surprisingly, Tannehill compares these two passages and arrives at this very point: "The things concerning the reign of God" of which Jesus speaks in Acts 1:3 include this revelation about his won role as the rejected and exalted Messiah, the king through whom God reigns."[18] The narrator's description of Jesus as the one who presents himself alive subsequent to his suffering thus provides the empirical proof for the initiation of God's reign.

Acts 17:2–4

This passage is one of the clearest examples of the narrator's summary of Jesus as the suffering-and-risen Messiah. Together with the following verses, the larger narrative segment interweaves diegetic and mimetic

---

16. Bruce, *Book of Acts*, 32.

17. The degree of narrative unity between Luke and Acts is not without dispute. While Tannehill (*Narrative Unity*, 1:xiii) and Tyson (*Death of Jesus*, ix–x) find complete narrative unity between the two works, Mikeal Parsons has argued strongly for a "restricted intertextuality" which he defines as "the relation of a text with other texts by the same writer" ("Unity of the Lukan Writings," 43). Acts, according to Parsons, functions as a sequel to the Gospel, not the second volume of a single narrative. This category does not, however, prevent "the interlacing of events, characters, and settings" between the two works though caution should be exercised when drawing interrelationships (ibid., 43–44).

18. Tannehill, *Narrative Unity*, 2:13.

materials with the narrator's comments in verses 2–4, introducing the focalized response of the Thessalonican "Jews" (vv. 5–9).[19]

Returning to the iterative mode, the narrator summarizes the content of Paul's preaching in the synagogues.[20] On at least three different occasions, Paul enters the synagogue at Thessalonica and sets forth his position on the basis of the Scriptures, "explaining and proving that it was necessary for the Messiah to suffer and to rise from the dead" (vv. 2–3). This oft-repeated message is an equivalent to the "preaching of Jesus" evidenced by the narrator's immediate elaboration in which Paul identifies this Messiah as "Jesus whom I am proclaiming to you" (v. 3). According to the narrator's categories, the proclamation about Jesus includes both essential elements of his death and resurrection in the fulfillment of his role as Messiah.

While the narrator invites readers to supply details of the summarized message by recalling previous sermons preached by Peter and Paul,[21] specific mentioning of the Messiah's death and resurrection directs readers to focus on these two elements. Because the narrator of Acts possesses a high degree of authority in relationship to his readers, acceptance of the summary seems accurate and reliable. The power of the narrator occasionally woos even the most skeptical readers: historical-critical ones. Ernst Haenchen, for example, when commenting on 17:3, ascertains "the doctrine of the death and resurrection of the Messiah Jesus" to be the "most important" aspect of Christian preaching portrayed in Acts.[22]

Also noteworthy, the position of the narrator in this key passage remains consistent with the initial image presented at the beginning of the book. Even though the "primacy effect" influences readers' understanding, the first impression does not act as a hermeneutical straitjacket. Given enough counter evidence, readers are likely to change their opinion.[23] Yet the narrator uses this summary as an opportunity to reinforce

---

19. Funk notes that introductions, conclusions, and transitions often contain unfocused narration (diegetic material) and "can occur anywhere, mixed with a more focused variety" (*Poetics*, 156).

20. Funk cites a parallel example found in Acts 9:19–20 (ibid., 158–59).

21. Both Tannehill (*Narrative Unity*, 2:206) and Polhill (*Acts*, 360) agree that the earlier sermons in Acts provide the details of the narrator's summary of the messianic preaching in 17:2–3.

22. Haenchen, *Acts*, 507.

23. Paul provides an excellent example of such a change. At first, the narrator de-

the initial judgment about the essential attributes of Jesus. In fact, the narrator brings the image into sharper focus by explicitly labeling him the "Messiah."

Furthermore, the mention of Paul's "opening up" (διανοίγων) of the Scriptures to demonstrate the messianic claims of Jesus echoes the Third Gospel, when the resurrected Jesus "opens up" the Scriptures for the same purpose (Luke 24:32).[24] The disciples on the road to Emmaus describe the risen Jesus similarly (διήνοιγεν ἡμῖν τὰς γραφάς) as they refer to his words about the necessary suffering and exaltation of the Messiah (24:26).[25] In a later episode, the risen Jesus "opens up" (διήνοιξεν) the disciples' minds to the Scriptures by explaining the necessity of the Messiah "to suffer and rise from the dead on the third day" (24:45–46).

Does the concept of necessity apply to suffering and resurrection or suffering alone? Charles H. Cosgrove emphasizes the suffering aspect of the divine "musts" when he notes the "eleven references to the necessity of Jesus' passion in Luke-Acts."[26] Yet later in the article, Cosgrove defines the "passion event" as inclusive of the "cross and resurrection/ascension."[27] Grammatically, both events are intimately connected with the divine imperative because the parallel infinitives (παθεῖν καὶ ἀναστῆναι) are both dependent on the impersonal verb δεῖ (Luke 24:46). Moreover, the appeal to Scriptures seems to support the necessity of both events. Though the issue will be explored in greater detail in the following section, note that when Peter and Paul appeal to the fulfillment of specific Scriptures, they include prophecies about the Messiah's death *and* resurrection/exaltation.

---

scribes him as one who heartily approves of the killing of Stephen (8:1) and becomes an aggressive persecutor of the church (8:3). But the counter evidence of his conversion and subsequent preaching activities should convince readers that a change has occurred. Nevertheless, the primacy effect is powerful enough that they may be reluctant at first to accept Paul's conversion as genuine, similar to the reluctance of the disciples immediately following his conversion (9:26).

24. Tannehill carefully identifies the connections between the two accounts (*Narrative Unity*, 2:206–7).

25. The phrase "enter into his glory" encompasses the resurrection event (cf. Dillon, *From Eye-Witnesses*, 141–43). Tannehill concurs when he explains that the reference "seems to embrace both resurrection and exaltation, with the emphasis on the new status of Jesus which results" (*Narrative Unity*, 1:284 n. 13).

26. Cosgrove, "Divine Δεῖ in Luke-Acts," 174.

27. Ibid., 188.

Abbreviated Comments

In a number of instances, the narrator associates the activity of preaching with one of following direct objects: (1) Jesus; (2) the reign of God; or, (3) the word (of God/the Lord).[28] Just as narrative "gaps" require readers to interact with the story by supplying necessary material missing from the text,[29] these abbreviated comments beckon readers to supply the missing details of the proclamation summaries. Although conclusions depend on the analysis of the characters' sermons about Jesus, hints from the narrator indicate a desire for readers to recall the message of Jesus's death and resurrection. The opening scene and the summary given in 17:3 reveal the key elements of Jesus's story from the narrator's point of view while the numerous abbreviated statements of the same message demonstrate its pervasiveness.

As discussed above, the narrator guides readers' interpretation by telling them in 17:3 that the "preaching of Jesus" is equivalent to the proclamation of Jesus as the suffering-risen Messiah. Elsewhere the narrator makes similar announcements, yet without explicit reference to Jesus's death and resurrection. In 5:42, for example, the narrator describes how the apostles daily teach (διδάσκοντες) and preach (εὐαγγελιζομενοι) Jesus as the Messiah in the temple and from house to house. Philip, when he encounters the Ethiopian Eunuch, preaches (εὐηγγελίσατο) Jesus to him (8:35). In another instance (18:5), Paul devotes himself to "the word" by "testifying [διαμαρτυρόμενος] to the Jews that the Messiah was Jesus." Apollos likewise argues with the Jews to prove (ἐπιδεικνύς) through the Scriptures that Jesus is the Messiah (18:28). In each of these examples, the narrator clearly identifies Jesus as the object of their proclamation. The narrator specifically mentions the focus of the preaching; that is, Jesus as the predicted Messiah whom the narrator identifies through the opening scene and 17:3 as the one who has suffered and risen from the dead.

The emphasis on Jesus being the predicted Messiah must find support from the Scriptures. For this reason, the narrator is careful to mention the inspired predictions, the "words spoken by the prophets," as an

---

28. The narrator uses the verb εὐαγγελίζω with some of these objects but also by itself to imply the preaching of the "gospel/good news" (8:40; 14:7, 21; 16:10).

29. See Iser, *Implied Reader*, 34–46. By encouraging readers to supply the necessary details, the narrator draws readers into the story, giving them a creative role. Nevertheless, some markers will be posted to "gently guide" readers without leading them "by the nose" (ibid., 37).

important element of the proclamation event. Philip (8:32–35), Paul (17:2–3; 28:23), and Apollos (18:24, 28) each depend on the Scriptures to demonstrate the fulfillment of the messianic prophecies in Jesus. In Berea, the recipients of "the word" examine the Scriptures daily to test the validity of the Christian proclamation.[30]

Connections also exist between the proclamation of Jesus and that of "the word [of God/the Lord]."[31] When summarizing the activities of those scattered due to persecution, the narrator draws a parallel between two groups: one speaks "the word" to the Jews, and the other speaks to the Hellenists also, "proclaiming the Lord Jesus" (11:19–20). Although the recipients change, the message apparently remains the same. Similarly, Paul proclaims "the word" in Corinth to the Jews and the Greeks by telling them that Jesus is the Messiah (18:4–5). For the narrator, proclamation of "the word" is equivalent to the preaching of Jesus.

The announcement of the "reign of God" (βασιλεία τοῦ θεοῦ) functions as another equivalent message.[32] The narrator first introduces the topic in Acts by describing how the crucified-and-resurrected Jesus speaks about this topic repeatedly to his disciples (1:3). Philip later "proclaims the good news" (εὐαγγελιζομένῳ) about the reign of God (8:12), a statement which parallels the proclamation of "the word" (8:4) as it is identified specifically with Philip's preaching of the Messiah (8:5). Similarly, Paul preaches about the reign of God in the synagogue at Ephesus (19:8). Listening to Paul's message, the people of the city "heard the word of the Lord." According to the narrator, Paul routinely speaks about the reign of God in his preaching (28:23, 31), a fact which Paul himself affirms when giving his farewell address to the Ephesians (20:25). Tannehill thus offers an apt description of the reign of God as concomitant with the rule of Jesus as the Messiah:

---

30. The comments made by individual characters in their speeches, which will be discussed in the following section, offer detailed examples of how exactly Jesus fulfills these messianic predictions.

31. Minert H. Grumm succinctly catalogs the usage of this phrase: "'the word of God' comes twelve times; 'the word of the Lord' ten times; then 'the word of the gospel', 'the word of this salvation', 'the word of his grace' (twice); and 'the word' absolute ten times—a total of thirty-six times in Acts" ("Another Look," 334).

32. In some senses, admittedly, the reign of God has more of a future orientation, but the concept remains attached to Jesus. Robert Maddox aptly surmises the event as "a present reality though it must also be consummated in the future" (*Purpose of Luke-Acts*, 186).

> The importance of Jesus' own reign in the narrator's understanding of the reign of God explains the brief summaries of the missionary message that combine the reign of God and Jesus .... These are not two separate topics, for God's reign is established in the world through the rule of Jesus Messiah. Thus the missionary message may also be summarized simply as 'reign of God' (19:8; 20:25).[33]

With Jesus playing such an integral part of God's reign, it necessarily includes the important aspects of his death and resurrection.[34]

Also contributing to the synonymity of these phrases is an overlap of Greek verbs and settings. Διαμαρτύρομαι, καταγγέλλω, κηρύσσω, and εὐαγγελίζω often take any one of the three direct objects.[35] The act of proclamation in its different forms also frequently finds common backdrops, occurring in either places of worship, while traveling, or in cities or villages.[36]

Recognizing the correspondence between these terms is certainly not a novel discovery. C. H. Dodd qualifies such phrases as "virtual equivalents."[37] Bo Reicke draws a close comparison between the phrase "spread of the word" and other expressions used to describe the expansion of the Christian message.[38] Ernst Haenchen suggests that the reign of God forms "the content of the Christian proclamation."[39] More recently, Beverly Gaventa concludes that the "speaking of the word" in Acts "consistently refers to the proclamation of the gospel,"[40] interchangeable with the preaching of Jesus and the reign of God.

The narrator likely alternates the terms to avoid literary monotony while keeping this message constantly before his readers. Both William Freedman and M. H. Abrams point to frequency as an essential element

---

33. Tannehill, *Narrative Unity* 2, 14.

34. C. H. Dodd identifies the reign of God "as coming in the events of the life, death, and resurrection of Jesus" (*Apostolic Preaching*, 24), providing a helpful assessment for understanding the concept in Acts.

35. E.g., 8:12, 25; 9:20; 11:20; 13:5; 17:3, 13; 18:5; 28:23, 31.

36. E.g., 5:42; 8:40; 9:20; 14:7, 21; 17:2–3.

37. Dodd, *Apostolic Preaching*, 28.

38. Reicke, "Risen Lord," 162–63.

39. Haenchen, *Acts*, 141 n. 2. He points specifically here to Acts 1:3; 19:8; 20:25; and 28:23.

40. Gaventa, "'To Speak Thy Word,'" 79.

Diegesis and the Messianic Model: "Telling" the Motif   23

for the efficacy of a literary motif.⁴¹ Freedman also highlights the importance of variability: the motif thrives on a "family" or an "associational cluster" of references "rather than merely a single, unchanging element."⁴² The abbreviated comments by the narrator provide a variability and pervasiveness necessary for the formation and consistency of a death-resurrection motif.

References to Jesus's Death Alone

Despite the emphasis by the narrator on both the suffering and resurrection of Jesus, some diegetic passages seem to highlight only one aspect of the double-sided motif. The following section considers two passages in particular which apparently place the accent on Jesus's suffering.

Acts 8:32–33, 35

In the midst of "showing" the conversion of the Ethiopian eunuch, the narrator interrupts the scene in verses 32–33 and 35 in order to offer clarification for readers.⁴³ First, the narrator specifies that the Ethiopian has been reading Scripture from Isaiah that describes in strong tones the suffering aspect of the Messiah. The quoted part of the passage ends with a phrase about how "his life is taken away from the earth" (Acts 8:33; cf. Isa 53:7–8).

At first glance, the resurrection of Jesus seems strangely absent, allowing David Moessner and others to build a case for the heightened significance of Jesus's death. Indeed, Moessner highlights this passage as an illustration of the "accent" falling on the suffering and death of Jesus rather than his resurrection.⁴⁴ He is careful to note how "Philip begins with the Scriptures of a suffering anointed one in declaring the present 'good news about Jesus' (8:35) which leads directly to the chamberlain

---

41. Freedman, "Literary Motif," 110.

42. Ibid., 124.

43. Sheeley classifies 8:32–33 as a narrative aside given to provide context ("Narrative Asides," 105). Verse 35 is a statement made by the narrator in the iterative mode that describes "durative" action; that is, a type of continuous action best "represented by a solid line" (Funk, *Poetics*, 159).

44. Moessner, "Church," 183, 187.

being baptized (8:36, 38)."[45] Though some suggest that the phrase "for his life is taken away from the earth" can be construed as a reference to the resurrection/exaltation of Jesus,[46] this interpretation is not overly convincing and necessitates allowing the weight of the quotation to fall upon the predicted suffering of the Messiah.

When the entire Scripture citation in verses 32 and 33 are viewed in light of verse 35, however, Moessner's position does not exclude of the resurrection perspective. The word "begin" (ἀρξάμενος), which is part of the narrator's commentary on the unfolding events, retains the inclusion of Jesus's exaltation as an implicit but faithful partner of his death. Verse 35 expressly indicates the suffering and death of the anointed one to be only the beginning part of the message. Using this text as the springboard, Philip explains the rest of the story. Though R. J. Porter speculates that Philip "continued to preach the gospel to him from the subsequent verses of Isaiah,"[47] most commentators agree that the content would more likely parallel the kerygmatic message proclaimed earlier in the narrative.[48] How would readers likely fill this gap? The narrator assumes familiarity with the LXX, but does this include knowing the specific passages that follow two and three chapters subsequent to the quoted verses, as Porter argues?[49] A familiarity with type scenes appears plausible,[50] but readers with the kind of recall Porter requires are quite incredible and therefore unlikely. Rather his "preaching of Jesus," as shown above, most undoubtedly includes the equally important aspect of Jesus's resurrection and exaltation. The chamberlain therefore hears and responds to a message that resonates with two notes of equal intensity: one supplied by the narrator, the other supplied by readers on the narrator's cue.

Acts 14:22

After Paul is stoned at Lystra, the narrator iteratively summarizes Paul's words of encouragement to the surrounding churches: participation in suffering as necessary for entrance into the "reign of God" (14:22).

---

45. Ibid., 187.
46. E.g., Tannehill, *Narrative Unity*, 2:111–12.
47. Porter, "What Did Philip," 55.
48. E.g., Polhill, *Acts*, 225 and Tannehill, *Narrative Unity* 2, 111.
49. Porter, "What did Philip," 54–55.
50. Cf. Alter, *Art of Biblical Narrative*, 47–62.

Diegesis and the Messianic Model: "Telling" the Motif 25

These afflictions, contrary to the opinion of Robert Maddox, are more than "mere annoyances, which a resolute Christian can easily endure."[51] Rather, the suffering is real, painful, and necessary. As Moessner clearly elucidates, soteriology hinges on Jesus's suffering, which the persecution of his witnesses continues to proclaim.[52] Conceding this point, however, does not negate the duality of the death-resurrection motif. Viewed within the larger context, suffering plays only one part in God's overarching plan of salvation. The other critical aspect of God's plan is renewed life, as Paul himself illustrates when he rises up (ἀναστάς) after being stoned and everyone's "supposing" him to be dead (14:19).[53]

References to Jesus's Resurrection Alone

Other hyperdiegetic passages seem to emphasize only the resurrection of Jesus. In two of the comments (4:2; 17:18), however, the resurrection or hope of the resurrection is only tangentially connected with Jesus while one statement by the narrator in 4:33 does specifically highlight the importance of Jesus's resurrection.

Acts 4:1–2

In these verses the narrator describes how the Sadducees become "much annoyed" because the apostles are "teaching the people and proclaiming that in Jesus there is the resurrection from the dead." This statement reveals that the disciples, who had earlier received instruction from the resurrected Jesus about the importance of his death and return to life, now obey his instructions by teaching the people about Jesus and proclaiming the possibility of a future resurrection from the dead. The focus of the latter part of the comment lies not with Jesus but with the people. Rather than enlightening the image of Jesus, 4:2 suggests the outcome for those who believe their message.

Nevertheless the narrator does link the phrase "in Jesus" (ἐν τῷ Ἰησοῦ) with "the resurrection from the dead." As Conzelmann testifies about the construction, the two phrases "belong" together, and "in

---

51. Maddox, *Purpose of Luke-Acts*, 82.
52. Moessner, "Church," 193–95.
53. This scene will be discussed in detail in the following chapter.

Jesus" becomes emphatic due to its placement before the other expression.[54] Because Jesus experienced resurrection from the dead, those who align themselves with this Messiah may partake of a similar experience. Arguably the accent falls on Jesus's resurrection, not his death.[55] The phrase necessarily implies, however, that death precedes the resurrection. One does not simply translate into an immortal heavenly state; death is still the gatekeeper. Moreover, the detailed content of the preaching in the temple voiced in 3:11–26 and 4:8–12 maintains the focus on both the death and resurrection of Jesus.[56]

Acts 4:33

In this instance, the narrator recounts how "with great power the apostles gave their testimony [ἀπεδίδουν τὸ μαρτύριον] to the resurrection of the Lord Jesus." In contrast to the previous passage, the narrator here focuses directly on Jesus, emphasizing his resurrection, though the act of "giving testimony/bearing witness" generally carries a more comprehensive message.[57] Nevertheless, the accent shifts temporarily to the resurrection aspect of Jesus's mission.

Yet again such an ephemeral shift does not justify theological extrapolations such as the one given by Haenchen when drawing his conclusions about this passage: "In the first place they [the twelve apostles] are the witnesses of Jesus' Resurrection. This for Luke is specially important: his theology has its centre of gravity in the Resurrection."[58] Rather the comprehensive nature of the actual testimony given by the apostles centralizes both the death and resurrection events (e.g., 10:39–43).

---

54. Conzelmann, *Acts*, 32.

55. Kilgallen, "What the Apostles Proclaimed," 246–48.

56. The following section provides detailed discussion of these intradiegetic passages.

57. The witnesses for Jesus in the book of Acts have specific characteristics and functions. In a narrow sense, these are the ones who empirically experience the resurrected Jesus and then testify to others about the certainty of this miraculous event (e.g., 1:3, 22; 2:32; 10:40–41). More broadly, these witnesses are those who have experienced Jesus's entire ministry, testifying to others through a comprehensive message about this Messiah (e.g., 1:8, 21–22; 10:39–43; 18:5; 23:11).

58. Haenchen, *Acts*, 163.

Acts 17:18

After Paul arrives at Athens, the narrator mentions that Paul is preaching "Jesus and the resurrection." The preaching of Jesus, as 17:3 makes clear, certainly includes both the death and resurrection aspects of his messianic role. The additional proclamation of "the resurrection" is ambiguous, possibly referring to the announcement of Jesus's own resurrection, or more likely, the preaching by Paul of a general resurrection. Redundancy lessens the likelihood of the first possibility, but the second option corresponds well with Paul's later claim to be on trial for the hope of the resurrection in a more general sense.[59] Emphasis on the double-sided nature of Jesus remains unaltered, though the raising of Jesus from the dead may provide the impetus for Paul's hope in a future resurrection for others.

INTRADIEGETIC COMMENTS ABOUT JESUS

On a deeper level within the narrative, the characters in Acts express details about the story of Jesus, which the narrator often summarizes. The interpretive weight given to one diegetic level or the other varies according to the literary theorist and the narrative in question. Tannehill argues that the narrator of the Gospel often saves the most important material for the main characters in their speeches.[60] Support for Tannehill's position arises from the fact that this direct speech, even though classified as a form of diegetic material, occurs within the decelerated focalized scenes. Rimmon-Kenan clarifies: "Acceleration and deceleration are often evaluated by the reader as indicators of importance and centrality. Ordinarily, the more important events or conversations are given in detail (i.e., decelerated), whereas the less important ones are compressed (i.e. accelerated)."[61] Although the rule guides evaluation, Rimmon-Kenan admits that it must be adapted according to the specific narrative being studied.[62] In Acts, as Sheeley contends, the narrator exerts a great deal of individual authority and serves as the authoritative interpreter for readers.[63] To fur-

---

59. E.g., 23:6 and 24:15, 21.
60. Tannehill, *Narrative Unity*, 1:7 n. 4.
61. Rimmon-Kenan, *Narrative Fiction*, 56.
62. Ibid.
63. Sheeley, "Narrative Asides," 102. Cf. Culpepper, *Anatomy*, 34–49. He suggests the narrator in the Fourth Gospel "serves as the authoritative interpreter of Jesus' words" (ibid., 34).

ther muddy the waters, the narrator may speak through certain characters in order to convey the details of an important point.[64]

Do the narrator and main characters share the same understanding of Jesus? Some argue that character speeches may reflect a different perspective from that of the narrator. Christopher Tuckett, for example, reasons that concepts expressed in Peter's speech in Acts 2 may differ from the author's (or narrator's) perspectives.[65] While narrators and their protagonists may hold contradictory views, they may also speak with the same voice and thereby form a unified message. C. Kavin Rowe makes a strong case for Lukan theological solidarity with Peter's views in Acts.[66] An analysis of the intradiegetic comments in Acts demonstrates a clear continuity between the main characters and their narrator, working together in their effort to tell readers about the essential identity of Jesus.

References to Jesus's Death and Resurrection

When the characters within the narrative recount the heart of the Christian message, the accent falls on both the death and resurrection/exaltation of Jesus. Both events form the crucial elements of Jesus's role as the Messiah. And the appeal to specific Scriptures supplies details that demonstrate how these two events fulfill the necessary requirements of God's "plan."

Acts 2:14–40

In this early scene, Peter recounts the saving event that has taken place through the death and resurrection of Jesus. He, like the narrator, depicts both aspects of the Messiah as a double-sided event, happening in accordance with the "predetermined plan and foreknowledge of God" (τῇ ὡρισμένῃ βουλῇ καὶ προγνώσει τοῦ θεοῦ) (v. 23). Peter explains the content in clear terms: "This man . . . you crucified and killed by the hands of those outside the law. But God raised him up, having freed him from death, because it was impossible for him to be held in its power" (vv. 23–24). The accent cannot be said to be on one aspect or the other. When Cosgrove comments on these two verses, he rightly finds an ef-

---

64. Tannehill, *Narrative Unity*, 1:7 n. 4. Boris Uspensky notes that such a blending of viewpoints is not uncommon, (*Poetics of Competition*, 52).

65. Tuckett, "Christology of Luke-Acts," 141.

66. Rowe, "Acts 2.36," 53–54.

fective summary of kerygmatic history voiced through Peter: "'Jesus of Nazareth—attested—delivered up—crucified and killed—raised' .... All of this took place according to divine plan."[67] Though Peter begins with the crucifixion, he ends with the resurrection. At one point Moessner, relying on verse 22, claims that the "delivering up/over" of Jesus is most closely related to the divine plan and foreknowledge of God.[68] Yet, Peter proceeds by emphasizing the resurrection event in the following verses through documentation with prophetic words. In verse 31, Peter explains how David "looked ahead and spoke of the resurrection of the Christ." This "looking ahead" has obvious connections with the "predetermined plan and foreknowledge of God." Moessner concedes here that "both the rejection/death and resurrection/exaltation of Jesus are placed squarely in the center of God's saving plan . . ."[69] He further observes that the scriptural quotations in the passage actually establish the importance of the resurrection aspect in "that plan."[70]

At the end of the sermon, Peter once again highlights the dual emphasis of the Messiah's role: "Therefore let the entire house of Israel know with certainty that God has made him both Lord and Messiah, this Jesus whom you crucified" (v. 36). The exaltation described in the first part of the verse recapitulates his earlier statements (vv. 32–33) about how God raised Jesus from the dead and exalted him "to the right hand of God."

Acts 3:11–26

The second intradiegetic message that tells about Jesus's death and resurrection occurs after the healing of the temple beggar. Moessner finds a strong emphasis here on the "rejection, suffering, and death," which are "singled out" as the key point of God's plan.[71] Yet Peter's comments seem to encompass a more comprehensive view of the divine agenda.

As Peter retells the story of Jesus, the apostle does describe him as the one "delivered up" and "disowned" by the people, but also as the one whom God "glorified" (v. 13). Such glorification entails the resurrection

---

67. Cosgrove, "Divine Δει," 184.
68. Moessner, "Church," 184.
69. Ibid., 185.
70. Ibid.
71. Ibid., 186.

event. Peter then reiterates the twofold event in the following verses: "[Y]ou rejected ... [and] killed the Author of life, whom God raised from the dead. To this we are witnesses" (vv. 14-15).

If Peter continues to emphasize both aspects of this salvific event, on what does Moessner build his case? Peter explains at a later point that the people acted in ignorance, and the suffering of the Messiah was a necessary part of God's plan "announced beforehand by the mouths of all the prophets" (vv. 17-18). The phrase "that the Christ must suffer" (παθεῖν τὸν Χριστὸν) occurs here and elsewhere in Luke's writings,[72] but such a statement does not necessarily move the accent to the suffering role of the Messiah. In Acts 17:3, the narrator uses this phrase to summarize Paul's preaching about the Christ but explicitly states that the Messiah both "had to suffer *and* [my emphasis] rise again from the dead." Again in 26:23, both ideas are tied closely together. In the Gospel, Jesus explains to the disciples that the fulfillment of the Scriptures mandates both the suffering of the Messiah and his "rising again on the third day" (Luke 24:46). In each of these instances, the fulfillment of prophecies occurs through both the death and resurrection of Jesus.

Not only do these other references suggest that 3:18 gives only a partial aspect of the fulfillment of Scriptures, the following verses recall the other part of the Messiah's role that likewise must be fulfilled. The "holy prophets from ancient time" announced that God would "raise up" a prophet like Moses (3:21-22). "All the prophets" spoke about the time when God would "raise up his servant" (3:24, 26).

For Moessner to argue that the accent in the latter part of the speech falls on the suffering role of the Messiah, he must hold the reins tightly on the meaning of the word ἀνίστημι when it occurs in 3:22 and 26. Yet, as Robert F. O'Toole points out, the verb demands more than a simple reference to the vocation of Jesus.[73] Three of the most significant reasons follow: (1) the Book of Acts "consistently predicates *anistēmi* of the resurrected Christ"; (2) the speeches typically end with references to the

---

72. Acts 17:3; 26:23; Luke 24:26.

73. O'Toole, "Some Observations," 85-92. J. Dupont has also suggested an ambiguity of meaning in these two instances ("L'utilisation apologétique, » 321). M. Dennis Hamm agrees with O'Toole's conclusion and offers further justification for interpreting these two verses as references to Jesus's resurrection ("Acts 3:12-26," 199-217, esp. 214). William Kurz likewise finds the resurrection meaning more persuasive due to its context ("Function," 19-22).

Messiah's resurrection, not his earthly life; and (3) the context demands at least a double meaning for the verb in these two instances.[74] Furthermore, O'Toole argues that the construction of the speech forms a chiasm that ties together the two concepts of death and resurrection into a single poignant recounting of the Messiah's completed mission.[75] Thus, Peter's telling of Jesus's story continues to highlight both his death and resurrection. Moessner's strong statement that "all emphasis in this second speech is on the scriptural or divine import of the denial/death of Jesus" becomes an overstatement of his thesis.[76]

Acts 4:8–12

While the "rulers and elders and scribes" interrogate Peter concerning the healing of the temple beggar, Peter attributes the physical healing and the blessing of salvation to the crucified-and-risen Christ. On this intradiegetic level, Peter summarizes the story of Jesus as the one "whom you crucified, whom God raised from the dead" (v. 10). In order to demonstrate how this event conforms to prophecy, Peter appeals to Psalm 118:22, which foresees the Messiah as "the stone that was rejected by you, the builders; it has became the cornerstone" (v. 11). If the rejection parallels the crucifixion, then the transition from rejected stone to cornerstone occurs through God's raising Jesus from the dead.

Peter links this twofold event with salvation. Just as the lame beggar had "been made well" (σέσωται), so also everyone else "must be saved" (σωθῆναι) through the name of the crucified-and-risen Jesus Christ. Peter's play on the word σώζω accentuates his point. He moves from the physical to the spiritual level to demonstrate the possible effects of the death and resurrection event. In this case, the soteriological impact results from a singular event with two sides. Both death and resurrection receive equal credit and the two must be taken together.

---

74. O'Toole, "Some Observations," 85–86.
75. Ibid., 87.
76. Moessner, "Church," 185.

Acts 5:29-32

After being imprisoned by the high priest and the Sadducees, the apostles experience a miraculous release and then respond to their accusers by recounting once again the story of Jesus. In this brief speech "Peter and the apostles" begin with the resurrection, followed by the crucifixion, finishing with a reference to his exaltation that is connected with the resurrection event. This "exalted" Savior is now able to "grant repentance to Israel, and forgiveness of sins" (v. 31).

The "release from sins" is effected through the crucified-and-risen Savior. No distinction is made, and the forgiveness is not related more closely to one point than to the other. Thus, the exalted "Prince and Savior" encompasses both the passion and renewed life.

Acts 10:34-43

While Peter delivers the Christian message to those in the house of Cornelius, he tells the story of Jesus beginning with his earthly life, his death, his resurrection, and his exaltation as the eschatological judge (vv. 38-42). When speaking about the Messiah's passion and resurrection, neither event is elevated above the other; both receive equal emphasis. Peter then ties the life story of Jesus to prophetic fulfillment and consequently to the plan of God. Those who believe in this predicted Messiah are able to "receive forgiveness of sins" (v. 43).

Acts 13:16-41

This intradiegetic episode is especially important because it shifts to the character of Paul, who maintains the position established by Peter and the apostles. After Paul's dramatic conversion, he becomes a key evangelist for the Christian movement. The narrator earlier recounts Paul's synagogue preaching of Jesus as the Messiah (9:20-22), but readers receive few details of Paul's proclamation until now. Acts 13:16-41 reveals the content of Paul's earlier preaching in the synagogues.

The apostle begins by reciting a brief history of the Israelite people and then explains how God "has brought to Israel a Savior, Jesus" (v. 23). When he recounts the story of Jesus, Paul focuses on his execution and subsequent raising from the dead (vv. 27-39). Each of these events takes place in accordance with the words of the prophets (vv. 28–29, 33). Through the combination of Jesus's death and resurrection, Paul proclaims the "forgiveness of sins" (v. 38).

Nevertheless, Moessner still centers attention on the crucifixion. He argues that the death of Jesus mentioned in verses 28–29 is at "the critical center of salvation in God's will" because the events surrounding his execution form the "climax" of all the prophecies written about Jesus.[77] Moessner bases his argument on Paul's statement, "When they had carried out (ἐτέλεσαν) all that was written concerning him, they took him down from the tree and laid him in a tomb" (v. 29). The phrase "all that was written concerning him," according to Moessner, becomes a solid justification for making Jesus's death the climactic point of prophetic fulfillment.

The "all" in this phrase does not, however, justify making the crucifixion the climactic point of fulfillment or "the critical center of salvation." The word for "all" (πᾶς) finds frequent usage in both Luke and Acts,[78] often demanding a loose interpretation.[79] The Third Gospel uses a similar phrase to describe the resurrection event. Jesus is astonished at those who are "slow of heart to believe *all* [my emphasis] that the prophets have declared!" (Luke 24:25). The two on the road to Emmaus were slow to believe Jesus had truly risen as the women had reported. Only after Jesus explained "all" the Scriptures and reclined with them at the table did they realize that he had "truly risen" (Luke 24:27–34). While the "all" may serve as a form of emphasis, the emphasis in 13:29 is most likely not on the crucifixion over against the resurrection but rather on the fulfillment of the Scriptures in general. That the "all" is not exclusive becomes clear in verse 33. Here Paul continues preaching the "fulfillment" (ἐκπεπλήρωκεν) of the Scriptures through the resurrection event. He explains that God "has fulfilled for us, their children, by raising Jesus; as *also* [my emphasis] it is written in the second psalm." Paul wants to clarify that both events occurred in accordance with messianic prophecies.

---

77. Ibid., 189.

78. Cf. Bachmann and Slaby, *Concordance*, 51–55 of the appendix. According to their count, the word in its various forms occurs 1,244 times, of which more than 300 are found in Luke and Acts.

79. Acts 9:35, for instance, records the conversion of "all" the inhabitants of two towns due to the healing of a paralytic. The "all" here undoubtedly serves a hyperbolic function to magnify the effects of the miracle.

Both events are tied to salvation. Paul identifies Jesus as the promised offspring of David whom "God has brought to Israel [as] a Savior" (13:23). In verse 26 he declares that the "message of this salvation" is now being sent out to "the descendants of Abraham's family, and others who fear God." After he has thoroughly recounted and justified both the suffering and resurrection of Jesus the Messiah, Paul proclaims to his listeners that the "forgiveness of sins" is effected through this crucified-and-risen one for those who believe (vv. 38–39). Notwithstanding, Moessner still argues that the "salvation" of verse 26 is synonymous with the "will" and "promise" of God in verses 22 and 23, all of which relate most closely to the passion of Jesus.[80] While Paul does mention Jesus's rejection and condemnation first, he does not stop there. He completes the message with the announcement of the resurrection event and then declares that he has given them the "good news promised to our ancestors" (v. 32). Then Paul connects the fulfillment of the "promise" with God's raising of Jesus (v. 33). He emphasizes both events in the salvific process, not one over the other. Both provide the necessary content of the Savior-Messiah Jesus.

Representing a different viewpoint, John J. Kilgallen appropriately recognizes a culmination of the speech's content in verses 38–39, yet misjudges the earlier part of Paul's diegesis by emphasizing only the resurrection aspect of Jesus's redemptive activity.[81] Jesus's death, according to Kilgallen, is the obstacle to overcome: "Though put to death (and thus apparently unable to continue his mission as savior), Jesus is immediately restored to life and to such a life that he is now able to bring salvation to people of every time and place, in particular to the Antiocheans of Pisidia."[82] Moessner's inclusion of Jesus's suffering as part of the divine plan corrects this deficient perspective which comprehends the death of Jesus only negatively.

Acts 25:14–21

The story shifts to a nonbeliever's perspective in Acts 25:14–21. Festus, a Roman ruler, explains his dilemma over the case between Paul and his accusers, the "chief priests and the elders of the Jews" (v. 15). The two par-

---

80. Moessner, "Church," 188–89.
81. Kilgallen, "Acts 13:38–39," 480–81, 506.
82. Ibid., 506.

ties disagree concerning Jesus, whom Festus refers to as "a certain dead man" (v. 19). Festus then relates that Paul "asserts" this dead man "to be alive" (v. 19). Festus provides a summary of the court proceedings, which revolve around the story of Jesus, his death, and supposed resurrection. His skeptical reference to the resurrection of Jesus is an appropriate perspective for someone outside the Christian community.

Acts 26:1–23

In his defense speech before Agrippa, Paul briefly recounts the story of Jesus, explaining Jesus's fulfillment of the words spoken beforehand by the prophets and Moses; that is, the Messiah would suffer and then experience resurrection from the dead (vv. 22–23). These prophecies appear to be closely tied to the suffering of Jesus, but they certainly encompass his resurrection. Earlier, Paul predicates his case on the "promise" made to their ancestors (vv. 6–7) and identifies that promise with God's ability to "raise the dead" (v. 8). Paul undoubtedly refers to Jesus, explicated with mention of the suffering and resurrection of Jesus in accordance with the messianic prophecies. Paul later hopes to bolster his case with further appeal to the prophets (26:27). For the apostle, these prophecies certainly include and centralize both events.

References to Jesus's Death Alone

The only noteworthy example of intradiegetic speech to emphasize the rejection and suffering of the Messiah occurs in the seventh chapter with Stephen's speech. Moessner and Paul R. House properly envision the "prophet like Moses" who experiences rejection and becomes a victim of murder (7:37, 52).[83] A reference to the Messiah's resurrection may be indicated in 7:37, with the possible double meaning of the "raising up" of the prophet like Moses, but such a reference proves quite subtle among the throngs of comments about rejection and murder.

Readers are challenged at the end of the speech when Stephen's attentive audience suddenly interrupts him before he can finish. How should readers fill this narrative gap? Would Stephen have continued like

---

83. Moessner, "Church," 187; House, "Suffering and the Purpose of Acts," 322. See also Moessner's earlier work, "Paul and the Pattern," 203–12, in which he discusses the suffering of Stephen in detail.

those before him to speak of the victorious resurrection of the Messiah? In verses 55–56, the narrator and Stephen's speech guide readers to just such a conclusion by presenting a vision of Jesus in full exalted glory at the right hand of God. The righteous one was betrayed and murdered (7:52), but he was also resurrected and exalted, a point to which Stephen testifies before he is finally silenced by his accusers.

References to Jesus's Resurrection Alone

In the speech before the Athenians and later before the Roman court official, Paul tends to highlight the concept of resurrection though the comments are either inconclusive or only indirectly related to Jesus's role as Messiah. The following passages do not alter the portrait of Jesus by such an emphasis but rather contribute to the general concept of the resurrection of the dead as a leitmotif.

Acts 17:22–31

Although Paul's remarks here about Jesus are invaluable, their contribution for the present study is less pertinent. Paul does refer to the "times of ignorance," the need for repentance, and the day of judgment presided over by the "appointed" one. The significance lies in this eschatological judge receiving qualification by his "having been raised from the dead" (v. 31).

Because the audience does not permit Paul to recite the story of Jesus fully, only tentative conclusions result. Earlier statements about "ignorance" refer to the Israelites' inability to recognize Jesus as the chosen Messiah. They also act in ignorance with their rejection and condemnation of Jesus. The Athenians likewise fail to recognize God properly; consequently they fail to worship God properly (v. 23). Like the Israelites and God-fearers, these pagan Gentiles need repentance (v. 30). Salvation, though not stated explicitly, is granted through the appointed judge—the one who has been raised from the dead (v. 31). Such a phrase includes both a death and resurrection, but further details of the story of Jesus must be drawn from previous diegetic comments or postponed for future verification.

Acts 23:6–10 and 24:10–21

Given the opportunity to defend himself, Paul focuses attention exclusively on the resurrection of the dead. He considers his hope of a resurrection "in accordance with the Law" which "is written in the Prophets" (24:14). Later Paul asserts this hope for the "resurrection of the dead" as the sole reason he is on trial (24:21). He does not recite the story of Jesus. This line of defense aligns well with his earlier defense before the Council (23:6–10).

Because Paul does not elaborate on the story of Jesus, this speech contributes little to the present study. Nevertheless, Paul's words do indirectly corroborate the significance of the resurrection of Jesus. Paul's emphasis on the issue shows the possible impetus of Jesus's resurrection for the apostle's confidence that others may experience a similar event in the future.

CONCLUSION

The vast majority of hyperdiegetic and intradiegetic comments include an emphasis on both Jesus's death and resurrection. Temporary shifts in accent on one event or the other serve to heighten the effect of each event. On the one hand, Jesus's rejection and suffering is real and significant, not simply an unintended setback overcome through the divine intervention of God's raising him from the dead. Moessner's work has served as a much needed corrective to previous studies, which have enthroned a Lukan *theologia gloria*, relegating the *theologia crucis* to a silent or counterproductive role. On the other hand, the resurrection of Jesus alone reminds readers of the importance of this element for proper definition of his messianic character.

Thus, the characterization of Jesus equally emphasizes his passion and resurrection.[84] Both the narrator and the central characters speak from the same perspective, creating a unified vision of Jesus as the one who encompasses both suffering/death and resurrection/exaltation in accordance with the Scriptures. The narrator outlines this perception in

---

84. In a letter of response to this chapter, Dr. Moessner voiced agreement that "[i]n terms of motif analysis, both sides are *equally* [his emphasis] important and emphasized. . . . [but] with respect to the overall plot of Luke-Acts, the death/suffering/rejection of Messiah and the repeat of that rejection in Acts seems to take on special prominence" (letter to author, September 29, 1993).

the opening scene and, in 17:3, darkens the lines of the initial sketch by clearly guiding readers to accept this double-sided vision as the norm for the "preaching of Jesus." Throughout the story, the narrator provides frequent reminders of this message's advancement. The intradiegetic comments meanwhile supply critical detail and support to maintain a clear portrait of Jesus as the crucified-and-risen Messiah.

In terms of Freedman's criteria for a literary motif, the diegetic statements about Jesus create a favorable environment for the creation of a potent death-resurrection motif. The frequency of the message along with its occurrence in significant contexts satisfies two of the essential criteria for a literary motif. Nevertheless, the diegetic description of Jesus does not by itself constitute the actualization of a motif. The narrator must also "show" the same message on a mimetic level, thereby creating a coherency on both layers of the narrative while simultaneously adding to its pervasiveness and potency.

2

Mimesis and the Major Characters: "Showing" the Motif (Part I)

The diegetic description of Jesus as the suffering-and-resurrected Messiah finds mimetic replication in the lives of his followers. The focused scenes, those which "show" the detailed unfolding of specific narrative events, portray the actions of the characters in such a way that the movement of these characters echoes the reported actions of their Messiah.[1] On the one hand, the leaders of the Christian movement participate in events that parallel the suffering and death of Jesus. Yet on the other hand, these same leaders partake of (or anticipate) resurrection-type experiences in accordance with the resurrection of Jesus.

This chapter examines the actions of three major characters to determine the degree of harmony between them and the essential elements reported about their Messiah. "Major characters" refers to those who appear in multiple scenes and/or deliver extensive speeches.[2] More specifi-

---

1. Funk, *Poetics*, 134–35. As noted in the introduction, Funk describes the focused scene as one in which "the narrator transports the listener or reader, by means of words, to a specific time and place, with participants present and allows her or him to look on and listen in."

2. R. Alan Culpepper identifies three types of characters in narrative: the protagonists, intermediate characters, and background characters. The protagonists "are the central characters, the characters whose 'motivation and history is most fully established'" (*Anatomy*, 103). Most would agree that Peter and Paul are the protagonists in Acts; that is, the "major" characters rather than mere plot functionaries. Stephen meanwhile is often seen as a transitional figure between Peter and Paul. Nevertheless he shares many of the important qualities of these other leading characters in Acts (cf. Tannehill, *Narrative Unity*, 2:83) and delivers the longest speech in the narrative. His importance therefore

cally, this chapter includes discussions of the focalized death-resurrection scenes involving Peter, Stephen, and Paul.

Parallels, symbolism, and reader response principles clarify whether the experiences of a character recall the passion and resurrection events of Jesus. The parallels consist of pertinent similarities in language, activity, and sequence found within Acts, and between Acts and the Third Gospel.[3] The symbols for death and those for resurrected life encompass ancestral and cultural symbols that were a likely part of the literary repertoire of Luke's first-century readers.[4] Reader expectations and retrospection further illuminate the texts.[5]

PETER: IMPRISONMENT AND RELEASE EPISODES

In the Acts narrative Peter experiences three different imprisonments, each followed by a forced or miraculous release. The imprisonments function as a type of death parallel to Jesus's sufferings, while the releases echo his resurrection. Peter's final imprisonment is the most descriptive of his incarcerations and therefore serves as the clearest example. Nevertheless, all of these scenes represent mimetic episodes that follow the pattern of Jesus's death and resurrection.

---

justifies his inclusion as a "major" character. Although characters such as Barnabas and Philip appear in more than one scene, they do not merit space in this or the following chapter because their speech is limited and their actions serve purposes other than support of the death-resurrection motif.

3. Though some have expressed concern over the abuse of parallelism, the method still proves valuable when certain controls are observed. Samuel Sandmel warns against the "extravagant" use of parallels between the canonical and extracanonical literature and the claims that are made about sources ("Parallelomania," 1–13). More germane to the present study, Susan Praeder advises that "critical responses should state openly their criteria for parallelism and the strengths and weaknesses of these criteria. Their task is then to indicate the proposed parallelisms, the arguments for and against these proposals, (if possible) a preference for or against this or that parallelism and the reasons for this preference" ("Jesus-Paul," 38).

4. For an explanation of these symbols please see the introduction. In addition to these two mentioned, the implied author may also create symbols which "can be understood only with the context of the particular narrative" (Powell, *What Is Narrative Criticism?* 29).

5. The scholarly work on type-scenes and redundancy is particularly helpful here (Cf. Alter, *Art of Biblical Narrative*, 47–62, 88–113; Anderson "Double and Triple Stories," 71–89; Burnett, "Prolegomenon," 91–109; Tannehill, *Narrative Unity*, 2:74–77).

Acts 12:1-19

Peter's imprisonment and release in Acts 12:1-19 provides the optimal starting point because this particular episode illustrates a significant number of ways in which the narrator "shows" the connections between Jesus's experience and that of his followers. Though Robert Tannehill does not explore the symbolic overtones of the passage, he does note the way in which the language and setting cause an echo effect with the arrest and passion story of Jesus.[6] The scene opens with Herod the king "laying hands" on some of the followers in order to mistreat them. These same words, ἐπέβαλον . . . τὰς χεῖρας, describe the desire of those who eventually capture Jesus (Luke 20:19).[7] Moreover the use of the verb ἀναιρέω ("to kill") in Acts 12:2 recalls the passion language in Luke 22:2 and 23:32. The execution of James by sword, with the specific reference to him as the brother of John (Acts 12:2), echoes the previous beheading of John the Baptist by another Herod (Luke 9:9). James thereby functions as a type of forerunner for Peter; his beheading is a dark omen of Peter's likely fate.

The verb συλλαμβάνω describes the arrests of both Jesus (Luke 22:54) and Peter (Acts 12:3). As with Jesus, Peter's arrest occurs during the season of Unleavened Bread and the Passover (Luke 22:1, 7; Acts 12:2, 3). Herod "delivers" Peter over to the soldiers just as Jesus is "delivered over" prior to his passion.[8] Acts 12:4 notes that Herod intends to bring Peter before the people, a detail that, according to Ernst Haenchen, follows the passion model established by Pilate in his presentation of Jesus to the people (Luke 23:13).[9]

All of the details of the scene lead readers to expect that Peter will follow the pattern of the passion story narrated in the Gospel. Yet Peter does not die a physical death. He does, however, fulfill readers' expectations through his symbolic death. Richard Rackham first proposed such an interpretation in his 1904 commentary on Acts, later supported by M. D. Goulder (1964), and most recently by Richard Pervo (1990) and Susan

---

6. Tannehill, *Narrative Unity*, 2:152-53.

7. Cf. also the synonymous phrase in Luke 22:53 which Jesus uses to describe the action of those who are arresting him.

8. The verb used is παραδίδωμι. Cf. Luke 9:44; 18:32; 23:25; 24:7, 20.

9. Haenchen, *Acts*, 382.

Garrett (1990).¹⁰ Four different images substantiate their claim: imprisonment, the night, sleep, and being bound with chains.

Imprisonment, as Othmar Keel documents, commonly symbolizes death in ancient Mediterranean culture,¹¹ and is therefore part of the symbolic repertoire of the author and early readers of Acts. Passages from the LXX lend support to Keel's findings. Psalm 107 describes prisoners as those who dwell in "darkness and in the shadow of death" (v. 10 nasb). Undoubtedly, many of those who went to prison eventually died or were executed there.¹² For the early Christian community, imprisonment continued to maintain a close connection with death. Rodney Reeves aptly notes Paul's equation of his confinements in prison with death itself.¹³ When writing to the Philippians about his imprisonment, Paul describes the situation as one that "conforms" to the death of Jesus (Phil 3:10). Reeves also suggests that Paul speaks metaphorically of his incarceration as a "'sentence of death' where God's resurrection power 'rescued' him 'from so deadly a peril' (2 Cor 1:9–10)."¹⁴ Thus, the description of Peter as one confined by chains in prison readily conveys the notion of his symbolic death.

The scene also occurs during the night (12:6), the time of darkness, another common symbol of death. Keel remarks that one of the primary characteristics associated with death is "impenetrable" darkness.¹⁵ Psalm 49:19 describes those who die as ones who "shall never [again] see the

10. Rackham, *Acts*, 174–75; Goulder, *Type and History in Acts*, 43–45; Pervo, *Luke's Story of Paul*, 44; Garrett, "Exodus from Bondage," 670–75.

11. Keel, *Symbolism of the Biblical Word*, 69–71.

12. Keel documents the not uncommon practice of leaving captives in dark prison holes or cisterns to rot (ibid., 69). This passive killing was accompanied by its more aggressive partner, death by execution. Those who hear Rhoda's report that Peter was standing at the gate respond by saying the figure must be "his angel" (Acts 12:15), an indication that they likely believe Peter has already been executed and they are now being visited by the apostle in his interim state which follows death. See Viviano and Taylor, "Sadducees, Angels, and Resurrection," 496.

13. Reeves, "To Be or Not to Be?" 286–87.

14. Ibid. While scholars have not reached a consensus on the exact referent for Paul's "sentence of death" (see Martin, *Second Corinthians*, 15–16), imprisonment makes good sense in the context. The passage also has another connection with Acts because Paul mentions his dependence on the "God who raises the dead" (τῷ θεῷ τῷ ἐγείροντι τοὺς νεκρούς). In a similar manner, the characters in Acts depend on this particular attribute of God for "resurrection" from their symbolic tombs.

15. Keel, *Symbolism*, 65.

light."¹⁶ Indeed the entire abode of dead, Sheol, is pictured as a dark shadowy existence.¹⁷ The ancient Egyptians likewise believed death to engulf the deceased in darkness. For this reason, they dedicated several chapters in their Book of the Dead to provide guidelines for the release of the person's soul into the brightness of the daylight.¹⁸

In the early Christian milieu, darkness continued to be closely associated with death. The Gospel of Matthew finds the concept of "outer darkness," an eternal death, to be an apt description for the destination of those deserving punishment (Matt 8:12; 22:13; 25:30), while the other Synoptic Gospels emphasize the complete darkness at the time of Jesus's death (Mark 15:33; Luke 23:44). The narrator therefore ties this ancestral and cultural symbol together with Peter's imprisonment to paint a picture of the apostle as symbolically dead.¹⁹

During his imprisonment, the narrator describes Peter as sleeping—a common euphemism for death. The ancient Israelites often drew on this euphemistic terminology to describe those who had died.²⁰ The early Christian writers likewise found the term "sleep" a useful metaphor for death. Paul recalls how some Christians have "fallen asleep" though their physical death does not prevent them from partaking in the coming reign of God (1 Cor 15:18, 50–52).²¹ In the Gospel of John, Jesus refers to the dead Lazarus as having "fallen asleep" (John 11:11–14). Even more significant to the present study, the narrator of Acts readily identifies death in terms of sleep. The kings "fall asleep" to rest with their ancestors (13:36), and the early Christian martyrs do the same (7:60).

Finally Peter's captors "bind" him with two chains (12:6). Not only does this action demonstrate the strict confines of his imprisonment, but such binding (δεδεμένος) also reveals further connections with death. Those who must endure a second death are "bound [δέω] hand and foot"

---

16. Cf. Ps 58:8b.

17. Cf. Job 17:13; Ps 23:4; 49:14; 88:6; Prov 7:27.

18. Keel, *Symbolism*, 65. Cf. chaps. 3, 64, 66, 68, and 69 in the Book of the Dead.

19. Because imprisonment and darkness were commonly associated with death in first-century Mediterranean culture, Luke's first-century readers would have shared the symbolic understandings conjured through the mention of these two images.

20. E.g., "Then David slept with his ancestors and was buried in the city of David" (1 Kgs 2:10). Cf. Deut 31:16; 2 Sam 7:12; 1 Kgs 1:21; 11:21; 15:8; 2 Kgs 8:24; 13:9; 2 Chr 9:31; 26:23; Ps 13:3; Jer 51:57; et. al.

21. Cf. 2 Thess 4:13–18.

and cast into outer darkness (Matt 22:13). Similarly Satan is "bound" (δέω) with a great chain and thrown into the abyss, an abode for the dead (Rev 20:1–3).[22] Moreover Peter's binding alludes to the process in Jewish culture for the binding of a corpse in its grave clothes. The same form of the word (δεδεμένος) describes the binding of Lazarus as part of his burial (John 11:44). The Fourth Gospel later employs δέω to describe the binding of Jesus after his death (19:40), demonstrating the ability of this verb to signify more than simply the confines of imprisonment. In Peter's dismal situation, these iron wrappings readily evoke the more somber image of linen constraints for the dead.

With the accumulation of this evidence, we can—within the symbolic world of early Christianity—pronounce Peter symbolically dead. Each of the images conveys the idea of death and thereby leads readers to visualize Peter in a deathlike state. He, like Jesus, has been "crucified" between two others (12:6).[23] The prison now becomes his dark tomb where he "sleeps," having been "bound" in his grave clothes. Acts 12:6 makes the additional note that "the guards keep watch" in front of his tomb (perhaps to prevent anyone from stealing his body).[24]

Peter's "death" becomes even more apparent when contrasted with the new life he receives. An angel of the Lord "suddenly appears"[25] and light fills the previously dark and lifeless "tomb." The angel, using an ancient form of pulmonary resuscitation, strikes Peter on the side to revitalize him. The heavenly messenger then "raises [ἤγειρεν] him up" while simultaneously commanding him to "rise up" (ἀνάστα) (12:7). In Acts, the aorist indicative of ἐγείρω predominantly refers to the raising of Jesus from the dead.[26] The implication: just as Jesus was "raised" from the dead, so now Peter is "raised" from his symbolic death. The command ἀνάστα likewise alludes to resurrected life because of the participial form of the Greek word for resurrection (ἀνάστασις).

22. Romans 10:7 clearly identifies ἄβυσσος with the world of the dead.

23. Peter is positioned "between" two soldiers just as Jesus is placed between two criminals, "one on the right and the other on his left" (Luke 23:33).

24. Cf. Matt 27:63–66. Luke does not include this particular detail in his portrayal of Jesus's passion, but the posting of the guards in Matthew's gospel proves an interesting detail for viewing Peter's "burial" though its inclusion is certainly not essential for the establishment of his symbolic death.

25. The same language is found in the resurrection scene of Luke's Gospel (24:4).

26. Six of the ten occurrences in Acts refer to God's raising Jesus from the dead.

Mimesis and the Major Characters: "Showing" the Motif (Part I) 45

The actions following Peter's "resurrection" echo the same types of activity and responses following the resurrection of Jesus in the Third Gospel, thereby offering further evidence that the release reads well as a resurrection experience. Peter leaves his opened tomb and makes an appearance to the disciples (12:12-17; cf. Luke 24:15-31, 36-51). Before the actual appearance, however, a woman reports that he has "risen" (12:14; cf. Luke 24:10). Like those in the Gospel, the recipients of the news refuse to believe (Luke 24:11; Acts 12:15). Both groups suppose the resurrected person to be something other than the actual person.[27] Both Jesus and Peter explain to their dismayed listeners what has happened (Luke 24:46; Acts 12:17), followed by a type of commissioning (Luke 24:47-49, Acts 12:17). Both Jesus and Peter depart mysteriously (Luke 24:51; Acts 12:17).

Not only do the parallels in the Greek language and various images evoke the notions of death and resurrection, the prominence of the spoken motif reinforces such conclusions about the episode. As the previous chapter documents, the emphasis on Jesus as the crucified-and-risen Messiah permeates the narrative (with special emphasis in the first half of the story).[28] The persistent telling of the motif encourages readers to see the motif elsewhere, particularly in the portrayal of the narrative's characters.[29] Peter's imprisonment and release in the twelfth chapter thus offers an excellent example of the motif in its mimetic form.

Acts 5:17-41

Despite an obvious degree of repetition, each imprisonment scene maintains a high level of reader interest by presenting the motif with some intriguing variations. In 5:17-41 the apostles experience symbolic death when the high priest and the Sadducees "lay hands" on them and put them in jail (v. 18). In addition to the implications of confinement in

27. In Luke, they perceive Jesus to be a spirit (24:37); in Acts, they think the one standing in the courtyard is Peter's angel (12:15).

28. Though the telling of the motif recedes into the background toward the end of the book, this comparative silence does not imply a negation or lack of narrative interest in the motif. The spoken motif, established early in the narrative, achieves a primacy effect followed by reinforcement at certain key developments in the story. The last section of the story therefore has little need to reiterate the motif through "telling," but chooses rather to provide emphasis through the "showing" of the motif.

29. Cf. Freedman, "A Look at Dreiser," 386.

prison, the text mentions an important detail about the time, "during the night" (v. 19). The imprisonment and the darkness of night suggest a possible implicit death, but a symbolic reading of the episode becomes more plausible due to the events that follow.

An angel of the Lord comes, opens the gates,[30] and takes them out (v. 19). The angel then directs them to enter the temple and instructs them to proclaim the whole message of "life" (v. 20). The apostles obey by entering the temple (a sphere of life) at daybreak (the time of life) and appropriately teach the message of life (v. 21). The stringing together of these images confirms their symbolic resurrection experience.

Meanwhile, the high priest and his associates send officers to fetch the prisoners from their cell. When the officers search the prison, they find no one inside this metaphorical tomb (vv. 22–23). Their mysterious report causes the chief priests to become "greatly perplexed" (διηπόρουν) (v. 24). The parallel in Luke's Gospel recounts a similar experience: after the women journey to the tomb and go inside, "they did not find the body of the Lord Jesus," causing them to be in a state of "perplexity" (ἀπορεῖσθαι) (Luke 24:3–4).[31] Just as the two men in dazzling apparel tell the women not to "seek the living One among the dead" because "he has risen" (Luke 24:5–6), in the Acts episode an anonymous person "reports" (ἀπήγγειλεν)[32] to the chief priests that the apostles (who have likewise risen) are "standing in the temple and teaching the people!" (5:25). Later in their response to the high priest, Peter and the apostles characterize God as the one who "raised up Jesus" from the death he had suffered on a cross (v. 30). Just as the earthly authorities could not keep Jesus in the grave, they now cannot keep the apostles in their symbolic tomb.

Acts 4:1–21

The first imprisonment scene in Acts, though lacking in details, provides a number of key elements that contribute to a greater understanding of the

---

30. The gates of the prison correspond with the gates of death found in Job 38:17 and Psalm 107:18. These gates serve to keep the dead within their proper abode. God is the one who can shatter these gates and cut through iron fetters (Ps 107:16).

31. "Perplexity" is the usual response to a resurrection experience. When Herod the tetrarch hears reports that John has risen from the dead, he becomes "greatly perplexed" (διηπόρει) (Luke 9:7).

32. Cf. Luke 24:9, where the women "report" (ἀπήγγειλαν) the resurrection event.

death-resurrection motif. The scene not only offers an example of Peter's experience of the motif pattern, but the inclusion of diegetic remarks by Peter also illustrates how the narrator interweaves the showing and telling elements to create a persuasive motif.

The scene opens by introducing the antagonists who are seeking to prevent the spread of the gospel message. This group includes "the priests, the captain of the temple, and the Sadducees" (v. 1). In Luke's Gospel, Jesus faces a strikingly similar group who likewise arrest him. The ἀρχιερεῖς καὶ στρατηγοὺς τοῦ ἱεροῦ καὶ πρεσβυτέρους confront Jesus (Luke 22:52), while the ἱερεῖς καὶ ὁ στρατηγὸς τοῦ ἱεροῦ καὶ οἱ Σαδδουκαῖοι arrest Peter and John (Acts 4:2).[33] Like those in the Third Gospel, this latter group "lays hands on" Peter and John and places them "in custody" (Acts 4:3; cf. Luke 22:63). The imprisonment again signifies a type of death for those arrested, and the darkness of the "evening" (4:3) strengthens the image of death and parallels the time of Jesus's arrest as well.[34]

Their confinement, however, proves temporary. The Jewish leaders only partially succeed in their attempt to assert power over the disciples of Jesus. The next day (v. 5), a time of light and life, the aggressors are powerless to retain the disciples or make any serious charge to prevent their release (v. 21). In this manner, they experience a symbolic resurrection. After their release, Peter and John report (ἀπήγγειλαν) to the others (v. 23; cf. Luke 24:9, 33-35).

Moreover, the narrator reinforces the message by interlacing this scene with other materials that emphasize the death-resurrection motif.[35] The imprisonment and release are interwoven with a larger mimetic scene, which portrays the healing of a lame beggar and its effects on those

---

33. Other than the substitution of Sadducees for elders, the lists are virtually identical. Moreover Luke overlaps the meanings for these two terms. "Elders" appears in some instances as a generic term for those who are members of the Sanhedrin (e.g., Luke 22:66), a council composed of both Pharisees and Sadducees (Acts 23:6). Because Acts 4:2 specifies that the present conflict centers on resurrection, the Sadducees fit the context better than simply elders.

34. Though the word "evening" (ἑσπέρα) is not specifically mentioned in the Gospel account, the event takes place at a late time, after the Passover meal, and when Peter can only be seen with the light provided by a fire.

35. Among others, M. Dennis Hamm argues strongly that the events of the healing of the lame beggar are closely interwoven with those of the following verses ("Acts 3:12-26," 199-217). Mikeal Parsons has likewise argued that the scenes in 3:1—4:31 compose a single cohesive narrative unit ("Christian Origins," 411).

who witness the event (3:1–4:22).³⁶ When Peter confronts his accusers (4:8–12), he focuses attention on the lame man who has been healed as the reason for their arrest and trial. The presence of this restored individual later silences their critics (4:14) and becomes the impetus for their eventual release (4:21–22). The significance of these overlapping scenes results from the plausibility that both the lame beggar and Peter participate in death-resurrection type experiences, giving a simultaneous emphasis on the motif.

The narrator also inserts two diegetic segments, 3:11–26 and 4:8–12, which function as interpretive commentary on the interwoven scenes. The entire narrative unit revolves around the one who has been "crucified and raised from the dead." The narrator thus successfully blends diegesis with mimesis to create a powerful narrative technique for highlighting the death-resurrection motif.³⁷

Directly following the restoration of the lame beggar and preceding the imprisonment scene, Peter identifies the source of the miraculous event: faith in the name of Jesus, the one who had been "killed" but now lives because "God raised [him] from the dead" (3:15–16).³⁸ After they have been imprisoned and before their release, the Jewish religious leaders interrogate them concerning the restoration of health to the lame beggar. Peter responds firmly, "[T]his man is standing before you in good health by the name of Jesus Christ of Nazareth, whom you crucified, whom God raised from the dead" (4:10).

Such strong statements tied directly to these scenes offer interpretive clues to the action of the narrative. Just as Jesus experienced suffering and renewed life, so also do those who place their faith in him. They follow the same pattern of death and resurrection, albeit in different forms. In this instance, the disciples, most notably Peter, are subjected to imprisonment but also experience release, actions that coincide precisely with those of the crucified-and-risen Messiah whom they are proclaiming.

---

36. This scene will be discussed in detail in the following chapter about the death-resurrection experiences of minor characters.

37. Funk notes that "mixed modes" may indicate that the "narrator has suffered a narrative lapse . . . or that the narrator is attempting to achieve some particular effect by deliberately conflating the modes" (*Poetics*, 139). The effect here is one of focalization upon the death-resurrection motif. For a specific example outside biblical literature, see Freedman, "A Look at Dreiser," 386.

38. For a detailed explanation of the hyperdiegetic material in 3:11–26, see the section on this passage in the first chapter.

The clarity with which the narrator reveals Peter's final imprisonment episode as a symbolic death and resurrection provides interpretive clues for the earlier imprisonment scenes (4:3–21; 5:17–41). As Janice Capel Anderson notes, "the implied reader reads each episode [of a "type" scene] in light of the other, in prospect and retrospect."[39] The portrayal of each incarceration and release of Peter therefore contributes to the meaning of the other. Each imprisonment scene presents the death-resurrection motif with intriguing variation, building to a crescendo with Peter's final incarceration and release.

STEPHEN: DEATH AND ANTICIPATED RESURRECTION

The extensive scene portraying the death of Stephen reveals a number of explicit parallels with the death of Jesus.[40] Both must go before the Sanhedrin (Acts 6:12; Luke 22:66); false witnesses testify against them (Acts 6:11, 13; Luke 23:2); the chief priests question them (Acts 7:1; Luke 22:66–67); both speak of the "Son of Man" (Acts 7:55–56; Luke 22:69); their listeners react with violence to their testimony (Acts 7:54, 57–59; Luke 22:71); both commit their spirit to God (Acts 7:59; Luke 23:46); and, both ask God not to hold these wrongs against their persecutors (Acts 7:60; Luke 23:34).

The obvious parallels abound, but the rationale behind their presence remains elusive. In the days of *Tendenzschrift*, Edward Zeller viewed the parallels as a method of using Stephen to form a link between Petrine and Pauline Christianity.[41] Charles Talbert, working from redactional analysis, contended that such parallels establish a strong succession motif; that is, the true successors of Jesus become apparent through duplication of events in his life.[42] More recent opinions tend to utilize the parallels as a demonstration of the major role of suffering endured by Jesus and his

---

39. Anderson, "Double and Triple Stories," 72.

40. These parallels have not gone unnoticed by biblical scholars. Cf. Zeller, *Contents and Origin*, 176; Dornseiff, "Lukas der Schriftsteller," 136–38.; Trocmé, *Livre des Actes et l'Histoire*, 186–87; Talbert, *Literary Patterns*, 96–97; Richard, *Acts 6:1—8:4*, 281–301; Moessner, "New Light," 227–34; and, Tannehill, *Narrative Unity*, 2:68, 99–100.

41. Zeller, *Contents and Origin*, 176.

42. Talbert, *Literary Patterns*, 125–36.

followers.⁴³ They become the rejected prophets "like Moses" who must endure much persecution.

The stoning of Stephen certainly exemplifies suffering, duplicating the pattern of Jesus's passion in the Third Gospel. Unlike Paul at Lystra, Stephen does not "arise" after his stoning. Following Stephen's death, they bury him and make "loud lamentation over him" (8:2). Consequently, his martyrdom vividly portrays the first part of the death-resurrection motif. The reality of suffering becomes painfully clear.

Is the second half of the motif absent from the Stephen episode? The narrator does not explicitly show the resurrection of Stephen, but hints of resurrection shine through the crevices of this dark scene. One particularly bright ray streams through as Stephen envisions heaven opening up and the "Son of Man" standing at the right hand of God.⁴⁴ In so doing Stephen is able to see the "glory of God" (7:55), bearing witness to the exaltation of the resurrected Jesus.⁴⁵ To this one Stephen commits his spirit (7:59).

The standing position (ἑστῶτα) of the Son of Man lends further hope for Stephen's resurrection. Why is the exalted Jesus standing at the right hand of God rather than sitting? In his trial before the Sanhedrin, Jesus claimed that he (as the Son of Man) would be "seated at the right hand of the power of God" (Luke 22:69). Three options hold the greatest possibility for explaining the reason for the upright position: (1) Jesus stands as a witness on Stephen's behalf in front of the heavenly court;⁴⁶ (2) the standing of Christ represents his preparation for the Parousia;⁴⁷ and (3) the exalted Christ stands to receive his faithful witness Stephen.⁴⁸

All of these interpretations create an atmosphere of hope for Stephen. The first option conveys the idea of heavenly vindication for one found

---

43. Tannehill (*Narrative Unity*, 2:97) generally follows Moessner, who understands the parallels as an indication that Stephen, like Jesus, is portrayed as "a type of the Deuteronomistic rejected prophets" ("New Light," 234).

44. In the Third Gospel, Jesus refers to himself with this title and the claim that he will be at the right hand of God's power (Luke 22:69).

45. Cf. Acts 5:30-31. According to Jerome Neyrey, the trial of Jesus continues through Acts and here bears testimony to the risen Jesus (*Passion According to Luke*, 97).

46. Cf. Luke 12:8, "And I tell you, everyone who acknowledges me before others, the Son of Man also will acknowledge him before the angels of God." Cf. Moule, "From Defendant to Judge," 90-91.

47. Owen, "Stephen's Vision," 225.

48. Conzelmann, *Acts*, 59.

guilty by a misguided earthly court. Such vindication certainly does not exclude the possibility of resurrection for Stephen. Indeed, total vindication would restore life to this one who has been unjustly martyred.[49] The latter two options also suggest that Stephen will not continue in the grave. Either Jesus prepares for his second advent to receive his faithful servants or Jesus stands to receive Stephen/his spirit immediately on his death (cf. Acts 7:59). In each of these cases, one may expect a resurrection of Stephen to eternal life with his exalted Lord. As such, Stephen's death and anticipated resurrection form the most extreme case of identification with Jesus's experience and become paradigmatic for all Christians who will die a physical death, awaiting the Parousia with the hope for resurrection from the dead.

PAUL: DYING AND RISING WITH CHRIST[50]

Several scenes with Paul echo the death-resurrection event of Jesus. This section of the chapter examines three specific occurrences: (1) Paul's conversion experience (9:1–19); (2) his stoning and recovery at Lystra (14:1–20); and (3) his shipwreck and rescue at the end of the narrative (27:1–44). These events give readers three different windows through which to see Paul as an imitator of Christ. When readers peer into these windows, the narrator shows them how Paul, like Peter and Stephen, follows the pattern of the crucified-and-risen Jesus. The inception of his ministry, the middle of his missionary activity, and the final scenes in Acts reflect critical points in Paul's story, depicting him as one who identifies completely with Jesus.

The imprisonment episodes involving Paul, however, prove little value to the death-resurrection motif. With the exception of the ordeal in Philippi,[51] Paul's incarceration is of a more permanent nature, extending

---

49. Just as God will not abandon Jesus at his death, so also Jesus will not abandon his followers when they die. Their resurrection may differ from that of their Savior, but they can look forward to resurrected life with Jesus and the one who is "God of the living, not the dead" (Luke 20:35–38).

50. I am borrowing the title from Tannehill's work on Pauline theology, *Dying and Rising with Christ*. The Acts narrative pictures Paul as reenacting the messianic pattern in union with his Messiah Jesus.

51. The imprisonment at Philippi focuses more on the jailer than Paul. The images for the apostle are muted and therefore inconclusive. The scene will be examined in the following chapter as part of the Philippian jailer's death-resurrection experience.

from 21:27 through the end of the narrative. This perpetual imprisonment therefore becomes the background against which the rest of the story takes place. Consequently, the narrator chooses not to develop the death-resurrection motif specifically through Paul's prison experience. Instead, his imprisonment serves as a striking similarity with Jesus's trial prior to the passion event, becoming one of the many parallels that will be examined in detail under the section on Paul's shipwreck and rescue.[52]

Conversion Experience: Acts 9:1-19

The Acts narrative contains three separate accounts of Paul's conversion experience. The narrator portrays the first account in 9:1-19 while Paul himself narrates the latter two accounts recorded in 22:1-16 and 26:1-18.[53] The second version depends on the first for clarification while the final account is adapted by Paul to become a metaphor for the Gentile mission.[54] Because the first conversion story about Paul provides the most detailed description of his experience from the narrator's perspective, the Acts 9 account becomes the most useful for illustrating the death-resurrection motif, forming the primary focus of the present discussion.

As early as 1904 Richard B. Rackham understood the conversion narrative in 9:1-19 as a death-resurrection type experience for Paul: "He is crucified with Christ, and the three days of darkness are like the three days in the tomb. But on the third day with Christ he rises from the dead in baptism."[55] Rackham's analysis, however, has not gained widespread acclaim. I. Howard Marshall emphasizes the literal-historical aspects of the narrative;[56] Hamm and Haenchen interpret the darkness and light sym-

---

52. Talbert lists nineteen specific parallels between Jesus and Paul prior to and during their arrests and trials (*Literary Patterns*, 17-18).

53. For a good history of interpretation for the three accounts and their relation to one another, see Gaventa, *From Darkness*, 53-54.

54. Hamm, "Paul's Blindness," 66-67. While Hamm interprets one telling of the conversion in light of the others, Gaventa separates the three accounts by highlighting the different emphasis in each particular version (*From Darkness*, 90).

55. Rackham, *Acts*, 133.

56. Marshall, *Acts*, 170. He notes here the naturalness and logic of the episode: "It would be an instinctive reflex action for Paul to close *his eyes* when he was struck by the bright light. On opening them he was still unable to see; this in itself would not be unnatural.... In his weakness he needed to be *led* by his companions and so came to *Damascus*. Here he fasted *for three days*, no doubt still overcome by shock and probably

bolism primarily in terms of salvation.⁵⁷ More recently, Mikeal C. Parsons has affirmed the depiction of Paul's conversion experience as a symbolic death and resurrection.⁵⁸

Despite the differences, the validity of one interpretation does not necessarily negate that of the others. The narrative can reveal messages on both a literal-historical level and various symbolic levels. Paul's conversion story may therefore literally refer to the loss and recovery of his sight while simultaneously referring to his movement from spiritual ignorance to enlightenment or from a state of death to that of renewed life. The present task is to determine the plausibility of reading the passage as a death-resurrection episode for Paul. In other words, does Rackham's interpretation fit within the symbolic parameters of the text?

Acts 9:8–9 describes Paul as one who "could see nothing," being "without sight for three days." Luke-Acts and the larger biblical context closely link blindness with darkness and, consequently, with death. In Acts 13:11, when Elymas the magician suffers the punishment of blindness, "a mist and a darkness" falls on him so that he must be "led by the hand" (χειραγωγούς). In a similar way, Paul must be "led by the hand" (χειραγωγοῦντες) because of his loss of sight (9:8).⁵⁹ Such blindness echoes the dark helplessness described in Isaiah 59:9–10: "We grope like the blind along a wall, groping like those who have no eyes; we stumble at noon as in the twilight, among the vigorous as though we were dead." In other Jewish literature, loss of sight has close connections with death itself.⁶⁰ For Paul, darkness has engulfed all the hours of the day; everything has become night.⁶¹

What are the symbolic implications of such darkness? Spiritual ignorance is certainly one possibility. Dennis Hamm accordingly suggests that

---

by penitence as the enormity of his action increasingly dawned upon him" (Marshall notes the quoted portions of the text with italics).

57. Hamm, "Paul's Blindness," 63–72; Haenchen, *Acts*, 323. Hamm does, however, note that a close relationship between Paul's experience and the crucified-risen Lord. At Damascus, he realizes that "Jesus is not dead but risen" (62).

58. Parsons, *Acts*, 128–32.

59. Hamm persuasively argues that Paul, like Elymas, suffers punitive blindness with both cases having much in common ("Paul's Blindness," 69–70).

60. Cf. Mishna, "Shabbat" 23:4–5. According to this passage, loss of sight is a necessary stage (associated with death) on the way "to the great world beyond."

61. Moreover, Paul himself makes an association of his experience with that of darkness (Acts 26:18).

Paul "must be converted from his condition of embodying Israel's blind resistance to the straight way of God."[62] As documented above, darkness also conveys the idea of death.[63] Luke employs this strong image specifically with the death of Jesus (Luke 23:44-45). Now Paul finds himself in the midst of deathly darkness.

Additional evidence corroborates the case for Paul in a state of death. As Rackham noted long ago, the mention of three days without sight parallels the three days of Jesus in his dark tomb (cf. Luke 24:46).[64] Another indication of Paul's lifelessness is that he neither eats nor drinks. The narrator draws a picture of him as one who is completely passive and immobilized: Paul does not see, eat or drink; he does not speak or make any movement at Damascus.[65] While Gaventa may rightly advise against accepting any one of these images by themselves as an indication of death,[66] the concatenation of death imagery builds a strong case for viewing Paul in a deathlike state.

In order to "resurrect" Paul from his deathlike state, the Lord must intervene through the sending of Ananias, who initiates relationship with Paul. After Ananias lays hands on Paul and speaks to him, a miracle occurs. Paul regains his sight, rises up, is baptized, takes food and becomes strong again (9:18-19).

All of these actions give the indication of renewed life for Paul. The return of his sight brings the return of light and life. The participle ἀναστάς is a cognate of ἀνάστασις, the word for resurrection, confirming that Paul has been resurrected to new life. The baptism itself also indicates a movement from death to renewal of life.[67] The taking of food, as with Jesus, becomes a proof of his resurrection (Acts 9:19; cf. Luke 24:36-43).

---

62. Hamm, "Paul's Blindness," 70.

63. For documentation on darkness as an image of death, refer to the previous pages in this chapter on Peter's imprisonment of Acts 12.

64. Rackham, *Acts*, 133.

65. In Gaventa's words, "The encounter renders him helpless and Luke's repetition makes the point inescapable" (*From Darkness*, 60).

66. Ibid.

67. Romans 6:3-11 gives particular emphasis to this point, describing baptism in terms of identification with the death and resurrection of Jesus. In Acts, baptism, usually associated with receiving the Holy Spirit, represents at the very least initiation to new life with the community of believers (3:38; 8:36-39; 10:47-48; 16:33; 19:2-6). Robin Scroggs likewise notes the close relationship in primitive Christianity between baptism and the concept of death and resurrection ("Baptism in Mark," 536-37).

Instead of passive inactivity, Paul becomes strong and immediately proclaims Jesus in the synagogues (vv. 19–20). Responses to Paul's "resurrection" include amazement (ἐξίσταντο), fear (ἐφοβοῦντο), and disbelief (μὴ πιστεύοντες) (vv. 21, 26). The Third Gospel similarly notes how the news of the Jesus's resurrection brings amazement (ἐξέστησαν) to his followers (Luke 24:22). Both the women at the tomb and later the disciples become frightened (ἐμφόβων, ἔμφοβοι) (Luke 24:5, 37) when confronted with the risen Jesus or news about him. And finally, the disciples at first do not believe (ἠπίστουν) the reports that Jesus had risen from the dead (24:11). The nearly identical responses at the very least commend the possibility, if not plausibility, of reading Paul's conversion experience as a death-resurrection sequence. In becoming one with Jesus, Paul dies to his old life and is resurrected to new life as a chosen instrument for the Lord (Acts 9:15).

Stoning and Recovery at Lystra: Acts 14:1–20

Previously, scholars tended to accent Paul's amazing recovery at the expense of his suffering: Paul's misfortunes "are quickly overcome . . . with full energy and vigour."[68] Tannehill therefore offers a corrective by arguing that the Lystra episode becomes one of the climactic points of the narrative demonstrating the suffering of Paul.[69] In its entirety, this climactic scene forms a microcosm of the messianic death and resurrection.

Paul, like Jesus, finds success in spreading his message to the people/multitude (Acts 14:1, 4, and 11; Luke 19:48; 20:19; 22:2), but faces opposition from the Jewish religious leaders (Acts 14:2, 5, 19; Luke 19:39, 47; 20:1, 19; 22:2, 4). As in the Third Gospel, the religious leaders move the multitude to violence, resulting in Paul's stoning and supposed death (14:19). His executioners then drag him outside the city, a zone for the dead.[70] Though Paul does not actually die, the fact that he appears as one who has died fulfills the first part of the death-resurrection pattern.

---

68. Haenchen, *Acts*, 434. He further explains the stoning at Lystra as one of the "occasional reverses" interrupting the "triumphal procession" of the apostolic mission.

69. Tannehill, *Narrative Unity*, 2:180.

70. The dead were typically taken outside the city for burial because the sepulchers and cemeteries were located outside the city walls (cf. 2 Kgs 23:6; Jer 26:23). Luke 7:12 provides a pertinent description of a dead man being carried outside the gates of the city for burial.

Paul's passion also fulfills the prophecy in 9:16 that he "must suffer" (δεῖ... παθεῖν) as a part of his divine calling. The word παθεῖν is closely associated with the passion of Jesus and actually becomes synonymous with his crucifixion (Luke 9:22; 17:25; 24:7; Acts 1:3). Paul, soon after his "resurrection," confirms that the event functions as a fulfillment of his predicted sufferings when he connects his stoning with the tribulations "necessary" for entering the reign of God (14:22). In a similar way, the resurrected Jesus explains to his followers the necessity of his suffering for his entering into God's glory (Luke 24:26).

Paul's "resurrection" occurs when he "rises up" (ἀναστάς) from his deathlike state (14:20). As mentioned previously, this participle is directly related to the Greek noun for "resurrection." In this instance, the usage of the verbal cognate demonstrates the solidarity between the experiences of Paul and Jesus. The disciples standing around him become witnesses to his "resurrection," and then Paul reenters the city, a sphere of life. Like Jesus, Paul encourages the disciples before he departs from them (Acts 14:21–24; Luke 24:44–51).

Shipwreck and Rescue: Acts 27:14–44

The final chapters of Acts portray another dramatic passion, death, and resurrection sequence. In this episode Paul is the primary participant.[71] Not only do the passion stories of Jesus and Paul occupy the same position of their respective narratives, they also contain numerous parallels with each other.[72] Both accounts contain predictions of suffering, journeys to and arrests at Jerusalem, appearances before the Sanhedrin, false charges, claims of innocence, and death plots.[73] Because of the many parallels, readers anticipate a fulfillment for Paul of the messianic pattern.

Yet Paul, like Peter, does not die a physical death. Instead he fulfills the established model symbolically, as narrated in Acts 27:14–44.

---

71. Susan Marie Praeder does, however, make the valid point that Paul is not alone on the boat and any interpretation should not exclude the others who partake of the same disaster and rescue ("Narrative Voyage," 48). Because it would be redundant to explain the shipwreck and rescue in both this and the following chapter, I will only explicate the episode as it relates to Paul. Yet, I do regard the other passengers on the boat as undergoing the same type of experience as Paul.

72. Pervo, *Luke's Story*, 92.

73. Talbert notes a total of twenty-two parallels along with specific chapter and verse references (*Literary Patterns*, 17–19).

Paul's dangerous adventure at sea fulfills the first half of the pattern. The shipwreck, which Paul experiences, is a "common ancient metaphor for death."[74] Both the Old Testament and the classical literature bear witness to the popularity of this metaphor.[75] Just as Jonah equates his watery fate with Hades (2:3–7 LXX), so also Jason and the Argonauts compare their passage through dangerous waters as a journey "through Hades."[76] Not surprisingly, Mircea Eliade finds the "waters of death" to be a recurrent theme through much of ancient Mediterranean literature. He understands these "waters" as "pre-eminently 'killing': it dissolves, it abolishes all forms."[77] The writers of 2 Samuel 22, Job 38, Psalms 18, 69, and 107, and Ezekiel 26 all make allusions to the deathlike qualities of treacherous waters, often equating them with Sheol itself, the abode of the dead. In the book of Romans, Paul draws a connection between the sea and the underworld when he substitutes the descent "into the abyss" for that which lies "beyond the sea."[78] The Apocalypse likewise paints a similar picture: during a time of judgment, the sea releases "the dead" from its grasp.[79]

Prior to Paul's disaster at sea, the sun is obscured, resulting in an extended period of darkness (27:20), a phenomenon that likewise occurs before the death of Jesus (Luke 23:44–45). The narrator then contrasts this darkness and its implications of death with the daylight (27:39), an image of life. The dawn carries recognition of a distant land, the haven of life for those swallowed up in the sea. Psalm 68 describes such a deliverance from the sea as a deliverance from death itself (vv. 20, 22). Paul's rescue from his watery tomb to the dry land (27:44) symbolizes a renewal of life, an implicit resurrection experience.[80]

---

74. Pervo, *Luke's Story*, 92. See also Keel, *Symbolism*, 73–75; and Ps 107:23–32.

75. The classical Greek and Latin literature provides a clear backdrop for the connection of death with the large bodies of treacherous waters.

76. Apollonius of Rhodes *Argonautica* 2.609–10.

77. Eliade, *Images and Symbols*, 158.

78. The quotation, originating from Deut 30:12–13, describes that which is "beyond the sea" as the antithesis of heaven.

79. Rev 20:13. Earle Hilgert argues that the mention of "death and Hades" in the following line provides an "explanation and intensification of the term 'sea', rather than a contrast to it" (*Ship and Related Symbols*, 49). So prevalent is the connection between death and treacherous waters, that the writer retains the image to describe the "second death," the oxymoronic "lake of fire" (Rev 20:14–15).

80. Walter Radl, after examining the extensive parallels between Jesus and Paul, concludes that Paul's shipwreck and deliverance parallels the death and resurrection of Jesus

Thus, when Paul suffers shipwreck in the storm-tossed sea followed by rescue on the shores of the island, one may quite plausibly read this event as a type of death and resurrection for him. Indeed, several scholars have made this exact conclusion.[81] Nevertheless this symbolic interpretation is not without its critics. The greatest challenge stems from the critique of Susan Marie Praeder.[82] She asserts that, contrary to the evidence cited above, narrative reversals such as shipwreck and rescue should not be read as types of death and resurrection.[83] For Praeder, the context is the determining factor.[84] Yet the motif established through the preaching of Jesus's death and resurrection provides a compelling context for Paul's experience, especially in light of the numerous parallels with Jesus and the images of death and resurrection.

As argued previously, one plausible reading does not necessarily negate the others. Paul's shipwreck and rescue can legitimately be understood as a portrayal of Paul's literal deliverance from disaster at sea,[85] a

---

(*Paulus und Jesus*, 227–49).

81. Besides Radl cited above, see Rackham, *Acts*, 477–78; Goulder, *Type and History*, 74, 101; and Pervo, *Luke's Story*, 92. The fact that each scholar uses different hermeneutical tools and lives in different countries and/or different time periods testifies to the force with which the narrative makes its point.

82. Praeder, "Narrative Voyage," 42–49. Some of her criticisms prove appropriate because both Rackham and Goulder attempted to force Acts into a highly structured system. In so doing, they at times appear as the prince's courtiers forcing Cinderella's glass slipper onto her step-sisters' feet. Such awkwardness, however, does not mean that all of their suggestions are without merit. Moreover the fluidity of the literary motif alleviates many of these problems while affirming the implications of the narrative with its many parallels and images of death and resurrection.

83. Ibid., 48. Praeder draws the following conclusion: "Saying that Paul's deliverance from shipwreck is his resurrection is the same as saying that Jesus' resurrection is his deliverance from shipwreck." Her attempt, however, to destroy the symbolism by reducing it to absurdity fails. According to her example, Praeder views symbolism as linear; that is, both objects are on the same level and therefore equal to one another. Yet symbolism does not normally equate two objects of the same value. Instead one object of lesser value tends to symbolize another of greater value (e.g., the flag as a symbol of the country). It would therefore be inappropriate to take the object of greater significance and claim that it symbolizes the object of lesser significance (i.e., the country is a symbol of the flag). In a similar manner, deliverance from a shipwreck at sea can imply or be symbolic of resurrection but resurrection is not symbolic of a rescue from shipwreck.

84. Praeder sees salvation as the primary context of Acts and therefore interprets the shipwreck and rescue as a vivid illustration of the salvation experience (ibid., 116–17).

85. Hemer, *Book of Acts*, 133–52.

Mimesis and the Major Characters: "Showing" the Motif (Part I) 59

graphic illustration of the salvation experience,[86] or a description of symbolic death and resurrection for Paul. The acceptability of one reading should not preclude the legitimacy of another.[87] The question should be posed in this manner: can Paul's shipwreck and rescue be read plausibly as a type of death-resurrection experience? If the evidence suggests an affirmative answer, the legitimacy of Praeder's "salvation" interpretation does not preclude the more symbolic reading of the episode.

In all three of these episodes with Paul, the evidence does indeed reflect, on a symbolic level, the important message of death and resurrection. His conversion, his stoning and revival, and his shipwreck and rescue replicate the actions of his savior. Through these events the narrator depicts solidarity between Paul and his crucified-and-risen Lord.

CONCLUSION

When the narrator shows how the story progresses through the characters of Peter, Stephen, and Paul, readers may discover how each of these leading characters resembles the one about whom they preach, the crucified-and-risen Messiah. While 9:5 alludes to the solidarity between Jesus and his followers, a description of their actions demonstrates vividly how this communion entails not only suffering but also resurrection/exaltation. The rejection and suffering is significant, as shown most poignantly through the story of Stephen, yet the passion by itself remains incomplete. The exalted Jesus stands to acknowledge and receive the martyred Stephen. Peter suffers imprisonment, but also experiences the joy of release. Paul moves from death to life in his conversion experience. He succumbs to stoning but then rises up from his deathlike state. He suffers shipwreck in the storm-tossed sea but finds life again on dry land. Hence, both suffering and renewed life are shown to be integral elements of those who follow the crucified-and-risen Messiah.

These mimetic episodes breathe vitality into the motif by thoroughly fulfilling Freedman's criteria. Readers' exposure to the death-resurrection message obviously increases with each mimetic reenactment of the messianic pattern, thereby satisfying the frequency criterion. As with the

---

86. Praeder, "Narrative Voyage," 116–17.

87. Praeder, however, seems to work on the assumption that proving the plausibility of one reading simultaneously negates the acceptance of other readings (ibid., 42–49, 103–4, 116–17).

diegetic occurrences, the message again emerges in significant contexts, at climactic points of conflict, and at the end of each major character's missionary career (i.e., within the narrative).

More importantly, the images, language, and parallels between Peter/Stephen/Paul and Jesus bind their own experiences closely to the one about whom they preach. In so doing, the narrator creates a strong coherency between the diegetic characterization of Jesus and the actions of his followers. In addition, by shaping Peter's imprisonment-release episodes and Paul's shipwreck and rescue to conform to the messianic pattern, the narrator satisfies Freedman's criterion of avoidability. These events certainly have a degree of cultural and symbolic attachment with death and resurrection, but they do not by themselves necessitate such an interpretation. The narrator, however, skillfully adapts these mundane events to illustrate a theological proposition, utilizing them as appropriate images and symbols to portray the kerygma in mimetic fashion. Thus the combination of diegesis and mimesis create a genuine motif in accordance with Freedman's criteria. Yet, as the next chapter will demonstrate, the efficacy of the death-resurrection motif reaches a greater height with the support of the minor characters.

3

Mimesis and the Minor Characters: "Showing" the Motif (Part II)

Just as several experiences of the major characters "show" the death-resurrection motif, certain minor characters portray the motif through their actions in focalized scenes.[1] In this way, readers may see the message of death and resurrection on both the forefront and recesses of the narrative stage. Certainly, not all of the minor characters undergo death-resurrection type experiences, but the fact that some key "background characters" strongly echo the twofold motif does reveal its pervasiveness.[2] The narrator satisfies William Freedman's successful motif criteria because the death-resurrection motif becomes "part of the total perspective, pervading the book's atmosphere and becoming an important thread of the fabric of the work."[3] The narrator creates this effect by including stories of minor characters who undergo actual death-resurrection experiences and by painting over the actions of some other minor characters with the colors of the messianic pattern; that is, the narrator applies to these minor characters the appropriate images, symbols, parallels, and language befitting the twofold motif.

---

1. For detailed distinctions between "major" and "minor" characters, see the introductory section of the previous chapter. Let it suffice here to define minor characters as those that make cameo appearances in one scene and/or have limited speech.

2. I am borrowing the term "background character" from R. Alan Culpepper as a fitting description of the lesser but still important role played by minor characters (*Anatomy of the Fourth Gospel*, 103).

3. Freedman, "Literary Motif," 125.

The stories of Tabitha and Eutychus fall into the first category because each actually dies and returns to life.[4] The second group of characters follows the messianic pattern on a purely symbolic level, moving from the figurative realm of death to life. The healings of lame people form the primary participants in this latter group.[5] Some conversion experiences likewise support the motif through their actions and, more importantly, their acceptance of Jesus as the crucified-and-risen Messiah. Whether their experiences are actual, symbolic, or tangential, all of these characters prove valuable to the development of the motif, contributing to its efficacy.

Devoting an entire chapter to the involvement of certain background characters with the motif also prevents them from suffering continued marginalization and complete subordination to their major counterparts. Susan Marie Praeder has justifiably complained that previous studies in Acts have produced "hero parallelisms" at the expense of the minor characters.[6] Charles Talbert, for example, draws on the miracle stories for the express purpose of demonstrating the continuity between the early Christian leaders in Acts and their mentor Jesus who performed similar feats.[7] Luke Timothy Johnson likewise minimizes the importance of the minor characters by focusing attention on the protagonists. When, for instance, he discusses the resurrection of Tabitha (9:31–43), Johnson labels the episode in the customary manner as one of the "Wonders Worked by Peter" and then explains that this and other miracle stories "serve to refocus the reader's attention on Peter . . . ."[8]

Though Talbert and Johnson both fashion legitimate claims, the minor participants, as Praeder argues, also deserve focused attention. Their

---

4. The debate among some scholars whether or not Eutychus actually died will be considered in detail under the appropriate sections below.

5. One could justifiably include the imprisonment and release of John/the apostles as minor characters in conjunction with Peter (cf. Acts 4:1–23; 5:17–41). Similarly, one could recommend the inclusion of those who accompany Paul in his shipwreck and rescue (cf. Acts 27:4–44). The case for reading these experiences on the symbolic level, however, has already been offered in the previous chapter. To do so again would only prove to be a lesson in redundancy. Moreover, these scenes tend to focus the attention on Peter and Paul respectively, not the minor characters. In the scenes with Tabitha, Eutychus, and others, the minor characters do command the spotlight albeit for a limited amount of time.

6. Praeder, "Narrative Voyage," 48.

7. Talbert, *Literary Patterns*, 16–22, 57–59.

8. Johnson, *Acts*, 179.

actions show how they too play a significant role in the development of the narrative with its accompanying motifs. In particular, some of these minor characters function in part to portray the message of death and resurrection so that the motif pushes its message to the borders of the narrative, complementing the depth already achieved through certain episodes of the protagonists and the previously specified diegetic passages.

ACTUAL DEATH AND TEMPORARY RESURRECTION

The minor characters who actually die and come back to life provide the most compelling parallel with Jesus's passion and resurrection. The stories of Tabitha and Eutychus illustrate this point. Both characters follow the messianic pattern literally. While some ambiguity clouds the certainty of physical death in the case of Eutychus,[9] Tabitha clearly follows the messianic pattern without the benefit of symbolism. The narrator then strengthens their connection with Jesus by using terminology reminiscent of his experience. In each case, the participant reflects solidarity with the experience of Jesus, testifying to the presence of the motif among the background characters.

Tabitha: Acts 9:36–42

The story of Tabitha offers the most unquestionable example of the messianic pattern being replicated by a "minor" follower of Jesus. The narrator specifically designates her as a "disciple" (μαθήτρια) abounding in "deeds of kindness and charity" (v. 36; cf. v. 39). The description of her as a disciple indicates that she is a key representative of those who belong to the local church.[10] Her experience therefore demonstrates most clearly how all the disciples, inclusive of women, likewise conform to the pattern of Jesus's death and resurrection.[11]

---

9. Even if one takes the position that Eutychus does not die a physical death, the images accompanying his experience substantiate the case for at least a symbolic death and resurrection. Moreover, the conformity of this story to the death-resurrection type scene guides readers to interpret the story accordingly.

10. Robert Tannehill notes how this passage and the previous one about Aeneas tend to focus attention on the church by describing Tabitha as a disciple and connecting Aeneas with the "saints" at Lydda (*Narrative Unity*, 2:125).

11. Tabitha is a double minority. She is not only a "minor" disciple in that she appears in one brief scene with no speech; she is also a "female disciple" (μαθήτρια), a *hapax logomenon* that serves to highlight her gender.

Verse 37 reports that Tabitha becomes sick (ἀσθενήσασαν) and dies (ἀποθανεῖν). After some preparation, they "lay" (ἔθηκαν) her body in an upper room. Similarly, Joseph "lays" (ἔθηκεν) the body of Jesus in the tomb (Luke 23:53). Despite her seemingly hopeless state, the disciples send for Peter in a nearby town. In response to their petition, Peter comes to Lydda and enters the room. After dismissing the others, he commands the corpse to arise (ἀνάστηθι) (v. 40). Hans Conzelmann argues that this Greek verb functions here as a "technical term for the resurrection from the dead."[12] The use of ἀνίστημι in the appropriate contexts certainly supports Conzelmann's findings.[13]

Tabitha's return to life becomes apparent when she opens her eyes and sits up. The reactivation of bodily functions serves as the evidence for her transformed state.[14] Peter then takes her by the hand and raises her up, a movement parallel to God's raising Jesus from the dead.[15] Just as Jesus "presents himself alive" (παρέστησεν ἑαυτὸν ζῶντα) after his resurrection (1:3), Peter "presents her alive" (παρέστησεν αὐτὴν ζῶσαν) to the others who consequently become witnesses of her resurrection (9:41).[16]

---

12. Conzelmann, *Acts*, 77. He notes in particular Lucian's *Alexander the False Prophet*, §24; and *Philopseudes*, §26. Alexander purportedly "in some cases had actually raised the dead" (ἐνίους δὲ καὶ ἤδη ἀποθανόντας ἀναστήσειεν), while Antigonus, in *Philopseudes*, reports that he knew a certain man "who came to life more than twenty days after his burial" (μετὰ εἰκοστὴν ἡμέραν ἧς ἐτάφη ἀναστάντα).

13. Luke 8:55, for example, explains that the spirit of Jairus's dead daughter returns to her with the result that she immediately "arose" (ἀνέστη). One could justifiably translate the phrase as "she immediately came back to life." Indeed Antigonus uses this exact form of the verb in his amplified description of the man who "came back to life" (ἀνέστη τὸν ἄνθρωπον) (*Philopseudes*, §26).

14. John J. Pilch, in his sociological analysis of illnesses, identifies the problem of the dead as primarily one of inactivity ("Sickness and Healing," 205). Both the larger Lukan and other biblical narratives document that a return of bodily functions often verifies a person's coming back to life from the dead. Jesus demonstrates his resurrected state by eating (Luke 24:41; Acts 10:41); the widow's son "sits up and begins to speak" (Luke 7:15); Jairus's daughter rises up and is to receive food to eat (Luke 8:55); a dead boy begins to breathe again (1 Kgs 17:22); and another revived individual "opens his eyes" (2 Kgs 4:35).

15. Though the typical verb for the raising of Jesus (ἤγειρεν) is not used here, ἀνέστησεν functions in the same manner. Because Tabitha has actually died, use of the stronger verb becomes superfluous for proof of her death and resurrection. The mention of her "raising" does, however, create an added solidarity between Tabitha and Jesus.

16. This action again corresponds with previous resurrection stories such as the time when Elijah presents the revived son to his widowed mother, "Look! Your son is alive" (1 Kgs 17:23).

Furthermore, both the preaching of the crucified-and-risen Jesus (2:22–36) and the news about Tabitha's experience cause many people to believe in the Lord (2:41; 9:42).

Eutychus: Acts 20:7–12

Eutychus likewise suffers death, or at least an apparent death, followed by resurrection to life (vv. 9–12). Though some scholars debate whether Eutychus actually died from the fall,[17] the concentric circles of narrative contexts commend reading the episode as one of actual death and resurrection. The Eutychus story first recalls the earlier episode of Tabitha, whom Peter raises from the dead (9:36–43). The slightly larger narrative circle including Luke's Gospel contains a similar story of Jesus's awakening a young girl from her sleep of death (Luke 8:41–56).[18] This episode is particularly important because Jesus refers to the girl's being asleep when she has actually died (Luke 8:52). The more distant, yet influential, story of Elisha's bringing a young boy back to life (2 Kings 4:18–37) again suggests the view that Eutychus actually died and was subsequently resurrected. As a collection, these similar accounts become a type-scene that guides readers in their interpretation of the event.[19]

Even if Eutychus has merely been knocked unconscious, the symbolism of the passage—the midnight hour, his deep sleep, and the downward movement—confirms that the young man is at least symbolically dead. Nevertheless these and other images in this passage have paved a hermeneutical pathway to a multiplicity of readings. The passage must therefore be carefully examined before accepting Eutychus as a positive example of a follower who replicates the messianic pattern.

The greatest challenge comes from Bernard Trémel and Robert Tannehill, who both look disapprovingly on Eutychus. Trémel sees a

---

17. According to F. F. Bruce, "It is impossible to be sure whether Eutychus was clinically dead or not" (*Book of Acts*, 385). Frank Stagg also notes the ambiguity, concluding that either interpretation is equally acceptable (*Book of Acts*, 211).

18. Both stories are reminiscent of the reference to Lazarus's being asleep when he too has literally died (John 11:11). Luke's narrator does not find it necessary, however, to make the point explicit as does John's narrator (John 11:13).

19. Cf. Alter, *Art of Biblical Narrative*, 47–62. Though variation within the type-scene is expected (52), the basic structure of the episode should readily identify it with others of the same type. In this instance, the story of Eutychus clearly conforms to the basic format of a death-resurrection type-scene.

young man who at first refuses to accept the gift of life imparted through the gospel message.[20] Even worse, Tannehill envisions Eutychus as a lethargic disciple, a representative of those followers who fail to remain alert and consequently risk falling victim to the "savage wolves" who eagerly devour such careless members of the Christian flock (20:28-31).[21]

The midnight hour obviously conveys the idea of darkness with its handmaiden death, but what about the light within the upper room? The darkness outside, according to Trémel, appears to be contrasted with the "many lamps" inside. He therefore poses the thought that Eutychus turns away from the light of the gospel message toward darkness and death.[22] While Trémel's suggestion proves intriguing, any conclusions at this point would be premature.

Besides the darkness, Eutychus enters into a deep sleep (20:9). Such an action prompts Tannehill to suggest a parallel with that of the earlier disciples who fail to stay awake in the Garden of Gethsemane (Luke 22:45-46).[23] Accordingly Eutychus becomes an example of failure to be avoided. Yet, as substantiated in the previous chapter, "sleep" in Luke-Acts also serves as a euphemism for death, which need not be taken in a strictly negative manner. Stephen sleeps the sleep of death, but as one who has died in Christ (7:60). Peter's sleeping echoes the death of Jesus and is followed by a symbolic resurrection (12:6-7). Moreover, in the Eutychus episode the narrator seems to evoke sympathy rather than criticism with the comment about Paul's lengthy sermon and the lateness of the hour (20:7).[24]

The fall of Eutychus is again ambiguous. His physical fall could possibly reflect his spiritual failings[25] or simply confirm his death through the image of descent.[26] What is of particular interest is the detail that

20. Trémel, "À propos d'Actes 20,7-12," 359-69.

21. Tannehill, *Narrative Unity*, 2:249-50.

22. Trémel, "À propos," 362. He comes to this conclusion by drawing a parallel between Paul's long speech (ἱκανόν τε ὁμιλήσας) in verse eleven and the many lamps (λαμπάδες ἱκαναί) mentioned in verse eight.

23. Tannehill, *Narrative Unity*, 2:249-50.

24. Similarly the theme of alertness is softened in Luke's Gospel when compared with the others. Luke contains only one mention of the disciples falling asleep (22:45) instead of the three times in each of the other Synoptics (Matt 26:37-45; Mark 14:34-41). Luke's narrator also evokes sympathy for the disciples by adding a noble justification for their sleepiness; that is, due to sorrow (22:46).

25. So Tannehill: "Eutychus failed and fell" (*Narrative Unity*, 2:250).

26. As Othmar Keel notes, the Psalms often picture the deceased as going *down* to

Eutychus falls from the third floor window. The three-story fall with the connection of death possibly echo the three days Jesus spent in his tomb. Thus, Eutychus may not be a negative example but perhaps an illustration of one who replicates the messianic pattern.

The events following the lad's descent argue against Tannehill's thesis. After the boy is "picked up dead," Paul goes down and embraces him. The apostle then assures the others that the boy's "life is in him" (v. 10).[27] These prophetic words reach fulfillment with his resurrection at "daybreak," the time of life. At that point, they take the boy away "alive" (ζῶντα) (v. 12). The ζῶντα here, like the description of the resurrected Tabitha (9:41), parallels the proof given for Jesus's resurrection (1:3).[28] If, as Tannehill contends, the story's purpose demonstrates the danger of lax discipleship, Eutychus should not experience resurrection. Instead, Eutychus should have remained in his punitive state of death.[29]

While Trémel seeks to buttress his reading with a justification for the young man's resurrection,[30] the positive perception of Eutychus as a disciple following the messianic pattern better fits the overall context.[31] Luke Timothy Johnson poses the appropriate questions to flesh out the emphasis of the passage: "Is it by accident that the story takes place on the first day of the week (Luke 24:1), or that it occurs in an 'upper room' (Luke 22:12; Acts 1:13), or that the disciples are gathered to 'break bread' (Luke 24:30–35)?"[32] The narrator also mentions that this event occurs during the season of "Unleavened Bread" (20:6; cf. Luke 22:1). Thus the entire

---

the realm of the dead which is itself located in the "depths" (Pss 22:29; 28:1; 63:9; 88:11) (*Symbolism of the Biblical Word*, 64).

27. Such an assurance is reminiscent of that given to Jairus when he learns that his daughter has died (Luke 8:50).

28. The Greek verb ζάω is used in all three cases.

29. Elsewhere, as the following chapter will show, the Lukan narrator vividly describes the permanent nature of punishment meted out to errant individuals such as Ananias and Sapphira (5:1–11) and Herod (12:23).

30. He suggests that the purpose of the scene is to magnify the power of Paul's life-giving words which break through the barriers of death: "C'est la parole de Paul qui transgresse les frontières entre l'espace de las vie et de la mort . . . ." (Trémel "À propos," 363).

31. Nevertheless, either reading—Trémel's somewhat negative view of Eutychus or a more positive understanding of the young man—supports the death-resurrection motif. In the former case, Eutychus functions in more of an initiate-type role where he first rejects the message of life but then later receives it. He still moves from a state of death to life, becoming part of the Christian community. In the latter case, Eutychus plays the role of a disciple who vividly illustrates his solidarity with Jesus.

32. Johnson, *Acts*, 358.

scene is heavily laden with Easter imagery. With this in mind, John Polhill aptly ventures that Eutychus becomes an illustration of Paul's Easter sermon.[33] As Paul preaches about the crucified-and-risen Messiah, Eutychus becomes an indelible reminder of the suffering and renewed life integral to the community of believers. Moreover, such a reading obviously conforms to and strengthens the death-resurrection motif.

LAMENESS AND HEALING

Some minor characters reinforce the motif by moving from a state of paralysis to one of activity. Within the social system of Luke-Acts, both the healing of a paralytic and the raising of a dead person signify not only a return to wholeness or "being" but also a return to activity, to "doing."[34] John J. Pilch, in his taxonomy of illnesses according to the social world of Luke-Acts, reveals that ancient Mediterranean readers located death and paralysis within the same category of the body, the "hands/feet" zone of "purposeful activity."[35] Thus, both the dead and the crippled suffer from the inability to engage in purposeful action.[36] Because the inactivity of death and the inactivity of being lame fall on the same "social map" of the body for ancient Mediterranean culture, these two types of "illnesses" would have been closely associated in the minds of the ancient reader.

Nevertheless, the healing of a paralytic by itself does not necessarily signify a death-resurrection experience. The event can be read simply as a return to purposeful activity with few other implications. In order to justify a reading of the miracle as a replication of the messianic pattern, other factors such as the language used and description of the healed person provide additional indicators of a death-resurrection type experience. In the Acts episodes, the narrator does indeed portray the healing

---

33. Polhill, *Acts*, 419.

34. Pilch, "Sickness and Healing," 208.

35. Ibid., 205. Pilch finds that the social world of Luke-Acts divides illnesses into three different body zones: (1) the heart/eyes zone with its function of "emotion-fused thought," (2) the mouth/ears zone as the base for "self-expressive speech," and (3) the hands/feet area with its primary function of purposeful action (203ff.). He defines taxonomy as the "identification, classification, and clustering of illnesses into culturally meaningful categories" (200).

36. Ibid.

of paralytics in this fashion, paving the way to a deeper understanding of the events.

Temple Beggar: Acts 3:1—4:31

The first healing of a paralytic unfolds in the third chapter of Acts. The key phrase, "Peter raised [ἤγειρεν] him up" (3:7), signals to readers that this episode may contain symbolic overtones; that is, the beggar's physical healing may be a reenactment, on a deeper level, of the resurrection of Jesus. The narrator and protagonists predominantly rely on ἐγείρω to describe the raising of Jesus from the dead.[37] Thus when the narrator refers to the lame man in an identical manner, the parallel becomes evident, lacing the two events together. Peter's explanation of the healing ties the knot securely by twice attributing the miracle to Jesus, "the one whom God raised [ἤγειρεν] from the dead" (3:15; 4:10).[38] For this reason, M. Dennis Hamm concludes that the healing becomes "a sign of the resurrection" and "a manifestation, and effect, of God's raising of Jesus."[39]

Such a resurrection-type experience, however, requires a previous state of death. The question must therefore be answered whether the temple beggar's paralysis and surrounding circumstances fulfill this prerequisite. As Peter and John approach the temple gates, they encounter "a certain man who has been lame [χωλός] from birth" (3:2). The semantic domain for lameness does allude to the idea of symbolic death: a state of weakness, paralysis, having stiffness "to the point of not being able to move."[40] The postmortem effect of rigor mortis leaves the beggar incapacitated and inactive. Such a state of passivity, as Marice Farbridge documents, accords well with the description of those in the abode of

---

37. Of the thirteen occurrences of ἐγείρω in Acts, six refer specifically to God's raising Jesus from the dead (3:15; 4:10; 5:30; 10:40; 13:30; 13:37), one is a general reference to God's ability to raise people from the dead (26:8), and five out of the remaining six occurrences describe characters who likely experience symbolic resurrections parallel to Jesus's own return from the dead (3:6, 7; 9:8; 10:26; 12:7).

38. Peter also uses ἀνίστημι (3:22, 26) here in reference to God's "raising" of his servant Jesus, further substantiating the resurrection side of the motif. Robert F. O'Toole builds a strong case for the double *entendre* of the verb in these two verses, referring both to the calling of the prophet and the resurrection of Jesus from the dead ("Some Observations," 85–92).

39. Hamm, "Acts 3:12–26," 202–3.

40. L&N, 1:272–73.

the dead.⁴¹ Pilch, as stated above, further substantiates these findings by locating paralysis and death as "illnesses" falling within the same "culturally meaningful category" of the body, the one pertaining to purposeful activity.⁴² In both cases, the patient is immobilized, suffering from the inability to function.

The temple beggar's condition also necessitates the service of those who "must carry him along" (3:2). The Gospel of Luke narrates a parallel activity with the description of a dead man who is "being carried out" for his burial (Luke 7:12). The lame beggar likewise has pallbearers who carry him daily to a place where they "set him down" in his plot (3:2). The same Greek verb, τίθημι, describes the placement of Jesus's body in the tomb (Luke 23:53, 55).⁴³

The spatial symbolism adds evidence to the verdict about the man's condition. He remains outside the temple in order to beg alms of those who are entering the holy structure. Temples in general, and the Jerusalem temple in particular, normally function as bastions of life.⁴⁴ The gate here serves as a barrier for the lame beggar who cannot enter this sphere of life on account of his condition.⁴⁵ Just as the dead man in Luke's Gospel was being carried out of the city boundaries, the lame beggar must also be separated from one of the specialized zones reserved for the living.⁴⁶

41. Farbridge notes that total passivity is one of the common characteristics attributed to the dead in ancient Mediterranean culture: "In the nether-world everything is in a state of inactivity and even decay. The dead are too weak to attend to their requirements, and must therefore be satisfied with dust as their food" (*Studies in Biblical and Semitic Symbolism*, 216).

42. Pilch, "Sickness and Healing," 200, 205.

43. As mentioned above, the disciples "lay" (ἔθηκαν) Tabitha's corpse down in an identical manner (9:37).

44. Keel, *Symbolism*, 122. The fact that Peter and John are on their way to the temple to pray demonstrates that the temple at this point in the narrative has not yet been abandoned as a place of God's presence and thereby a place of life (See Tannehill, *Narrative Unity*, 2:52). Later the apostles appropriately will preach the message of "life" there (Acts 5:20).

45. Polhill rightly recognizes the gate as a barrier established to prevent the lame beggar's entrance (*Acts*, 128). Gates also frequently become a place where judgment occurs, especially capital punishment (cf. the following note).

46. The dead were typically taken outside the city for their burial (cf. 2 Kgs 23:6) and capital punishment normally occurred beyond the enclosed areas of the community (cf. Lev 24:23; 1 Kgs 21:13; John 19:20). 2 Chronicles 23:14–15 demonstrates clearly the desire to protect the special zones of life from the contamination of human death. Jehoiada orders Athaliah to be taken out of the temple area before the soldiers put her to

Placed in this spatial and cultural context of death, the beggar's condition—χωλός (i.e., being "lame," 3:2)—can readily function as a pun, alluding to κῶλον (i.e., being "a corpse").[47]

The subsequent images of resurrected life contrast dramatically with the lame man's previous state. After Peter invokes the name of Jesus Christ and "raises" (ἤγειρεν) him up (3:7), the beggar changes from passivity to activity: he leaps, stands upright, and walks (3:7–8). Words of praise replace his anxious petition for alms (3:8–9). These new uplifting words, as documented by Psalm 115:18, indicate that he has changed realms: "The dead do not praise the Lord, nor do any that go down into silence. But we [i.e., those in the world of the living] will bless the Lord . . ." Instead of remaining outside, he enters the temple, the sphere of life, and makes his resurrection appearance (3:9). His presence serves as physical evidence of his resurrection, with the result that the people are amazed (3:10–11; 4:21; cf. Luke 24:37, 41). In this context, the reference to the man's age in 4:22, "more than forty years old," echoes the forty days that Jesus spends presenting himself alive with "many convincing proofs" (1:3).

The healing therefore closely parallels the death and resurrection of Jesus. The fact that these two events are woven together in a particular sequence also proves important. The alternation of showing the miracle (mimesis) and telling about its source (diegesis) prompts Mikeal Parsons to suggest that the central message of the traditional kerygma (i.e., the crucified-and-risen Jesus) becomes the "inner frame" of the scene which serves as the basis for interpreting the "outer frame," the healing of the lame man.[48] Not only is Jesus the source of the healing, but his experience of death and resurrection also strongly influences the interpretation of the lame beggar's transformation. Therefore, the entire scene—its parallels, symbolism, images, and sequencing—guides the reader to understand the healing as a type of resurrection from a previous deathlike state.

---

death. In accordance with his command they drag her out and execute her at the Horse Gate. Though beyond the parameters of the Lukan narratives, Hebrews 13:12 gives a particularly appropriate example with the mention of Jesus's death "suffered *outside the gate*" (emphasis added).

47. Read in this light, he has been "a corpse since his birth."
48. Parsons, "Christian Origins," 412.

Aeneas: Acts 9:32–35

Peter encounters another lame man when he visits the "saints" in Lydda. The story is quite brief, but echoes the earlier narrative about the temple beggar. Both were paralyzed and both receive healing through invocation of the name Jesus Christ. Due to the similarity between these two events, the first healing episode has hermeneutical significance for the second miracle. As Janice Capel Anderson explains, double and triple stories influence the reader's interpretation: "The implied reader's response is guided by the arrangement. The first occurrence anticipates the second (and third) and the latter recalls the former. The implied reader reads each episode in light of the other, in prospect and retrospect."[49] Therefore, because the first detailed healing reflects a type of death-resurrection experience, the second likely has the same connotations. Aeneas, like the previous lame man, moves from paralysis to activity, from symbolic death to renewed life.

Moreover, the source of Aeneas's healing is the same as that of the lame beggar at the temple. Both make their dramatic transformations through "Jesus Christ" (3:6; 9:34). As substantiated above, the first account clarifies the essential character of Jesus; that is, the one who was crucified but later raised from the dead (3:12–15). The narrator finds it unnecessary to reiterate the details here. Instead readers simply recall the sermon from the previous episode. The effects remain the same. The essence of Jesus's character becomes evident as it blossoms in the (new) life of the paralytic.

The placement of Aeneas's story next to the Tabitha episode also proves important. Robert Tannehill notes the Lukan narrator's propensity for linking male and female stories with similar messages.[50] The cumulative effect is one of intensification, "making clear that the two versions are to be understood as parallel."[51] In this particular case, the death and resurrection of Tabitha tends to clarify the deeper meaning of Aeneas's healing. He, like Tabitha, moves from death to life.

---

49. Anderson, "Double and Triple Stories," 71–89. Note that Anderson's "double" and "triple" stories are virtually identical to Robert Alter's "type-scene" (*Art*, 47–62).

50. Tannehill, *Narrative Unity*, 1:132–35. One example comes at the beginning of the Gospel with Simeon (Luke 2:25–35) and Anna (Luke 2:36–38), who both bless the baby Jesus and another pertinent example surfaces with the resurrection stories of the widow's only son (Luke 7:12–15) and Jairus's only daughter (Luke 8:41–55).

51. Ibid., 132–33.

Beyond these influential factors, Peter's commands and the responses to these commands give further evidence that the healing alludes to a symbolic resurrection from the dead. Peter first commands him to arise (ἀνάστηθι) (9:34), an imperative which parallels exactly his command given to Tabitha's corpse (v. 40). Aeneas responds to the command by rising immediately (καὶ εὐθέως ἀνέστη), which parallels the response of Jairus's daughter when she is resurrected from the dead (καί ἀνέστη παραχρῆμα) (Luke 8:54). Moreover, as documented above, the verb ἀνίστημι is closely related to the resurrection event.[52]

Peter's second command for Aeneas to make his bed (v. 34) becomes a proof of his renewed life analogous to the proof Jesus gives of his own resurrection.[53] Aeneas demonstrates the fact that he has returned to the realm of the living through a restoration of his activity.[54] The people respond accordingly by "turning to the Lord" (9:35), just as others do when they hear about Tabitha's resurrection (v. 42).

Lame Man of Lystra: Acts 14:8–11

As with the second healing of a paralytic, this third instance relies on the former occurrences to elucidate its meaning(s). Particularly strong parallels exist between the first and third events, serving to tie the two episodes together. Each paralytic is "lame from birth" (3:2; 14:8). Each is subject to the "fixed gaze" of his healer (3:4; 14:9). Each one responds to the command of his healer by leaping and walking (3:8; 14:10). Each miracle results in confusion and deathly repercussions for the healers (4:1–3; 14:19).[55]

The Lystra healing also has some common elements with the Aeneas episode. Of most significance is the command to arise (ἀνάστηθι, 9:34;

---

52. Conzelmann, *Acts*, 77.

53. Conzelmann notes that the command "serves as a demonstration that the healing has taken place" (ibid., 76). More intriguing, the object of the command must be supplied from the context. "Table" fits the context just as well as "bed." If we fill the gap with "table," the command becomes "Get yourself something to eat!" (a likely possibility suggested by Bruce, *Book of Acts*, 198). Such a command accords well with the proof offered by Jesus for his resurrection (Luke 24:41–43; cf. 8:55). However the command is understood, it clearly demonstrates a return to purposeful activity.

54. Cf. Pilch, "Sickness and Healing," 205.

55. In the first instance, the religious authorities have Peter and John put into prison. In the latter case, the Jews from Antioch and Iconium move the multitude to stone Paul.

14:10), which is the same command Peter gives to Tabitha (9:40). Just as Tabitha rises up from the dead, these paralytics rise up from their death-like state.

In all three healing stories, each undergoes a similar transformation: from weakness to strength, paralysis to movement, passivity to activity, and depths to heights. Reading one episode in light of the other makes clear that the healings represent something deeper than a person's gaining the ability to walk. Each one, with the exception of the last, is explicitly connected with the crucified-and-risen Jesus. Even in the latter case, Paul has been preaching the "gospel" (14:7), which necessarily entails Jesus as the central kerygmatic element.[56] Furthermore, readers of Acts naturally supply the source of the healing from their knowledge of the two earlier episodes.[57] The connection with the crucified-and-risen Jesus provides the framework for interpreting these events, leading to deeper levels of meaning beyond a return of their ability to walk.

The combination of the three paralytic scenes, therefore, reflects how the death-resurrection motif applies to different individuals in their particular circumstances. In the first and third cases, their participation in the pattern demonstrates an initiation into the Christian community. Because Aeneas is likely a member of the Christian community already,[58] his experience marks the continuing solidarity of the believers with Jesus Christ. The third miracle also exemplifies the power of the message to overcome racial barriers because this healing has a Gentile as its subject.

CONVERSION—THE CASE OF CORNELIUS: ACTS 10:1–48

The minor characters in Acts who experience a conversion often perform multiple functions within the narrative, creating a complexity that tends to obscure the mimetic presence of the death-resurrection motif. Moreover, with the exception of Paul's initial experience, the narrator has

---

56. Cf. Chapter 1 discussion about the equivalency of "preaching the gospel" and the proclamation of the crucified-risen Jesus.

57. Indeed the Western text becomes an excellent example of this gap-filling process by its adding the phrase "in the name of the Lord Jesus Christ" to the healing command.

58. Tannehill notes that the Aeneas story, coupled with the Tabitha episode, tends to focus attention on life within the Christian community by specifically connecting Aeneas with the "saints" at Lydda (*Narrative Unity*, 2:125).

Mimesis and the Minor Characters: "Showing" the Motif (Part II) 75

little interest in providing the detailed imagery, language, or proper sequencing necessary for a lucid portrayal of symbolic death and resurrection among the conversion characters. Nevertheless, these scenes prove important to the development of the motif because they have a tendency to focus attention on the convert's acceptance of Jesus as the crucified-and-risen Messiah, thereby forming solidarity with him. The Cornelius episode, being the most extensive, best illustrates the role of conversion in the advancement of the motif.

As stated above, conversion scenes offer a rich assortment of materials, serving a variety of purposes. According to Ernst Haenchen, the primary purpose of Cornelius's conversion is to show that "God instigated the mission to the Gentiles."[59] Philip Esler further specifies that the episode in its entirety offers a legitimization of the "table-fellowship between Jew and Gentile within the Christian community," which makes the Gentile mission possible.[60] On a secondary level, however, Cornelius has another purpose: to reveal the crucial role of the messianic pattern within the conversion process.

Unlike the blanket of animals lowered to Peter (10:11), salvation does not suddenly drop out of the sky onto Cornelius. Instead the narrator prefaces his conversion with hints of death/resurrection images and language, ties his salvation to belief in the crucified-and-risen Messiah, solidifies the relationship between Cornelius and this Messiah through the Holy Spirit, and seals his entrance into the community of believers through baptism "in the name of Jesus." Cornelius's conversion therefore reflects strong solidarity with the Messiah's essential character.

The heart of the conversion scene (10:24–48) opens with a symbolic, though brief, enactment of Cornelius's death and resurrection, foreshadowing the content of the actual conversion process. When Peter enters the house, Cornelius falls down at his feet(πεσὼν ἐπι τοὺς πόδας, v. 25). Not only does Cornelius's low position allude to the depths of the grave, the wording strongly recalls the fatal posture of two others at Peter's feet. Ananias and Sapphira both fall down dead before the same apostle (πεσών and ἔπεσεν . . . τοὺς πόδας αὐτου, respectively in 5:5, 10). For Cornelius, however, this deathlike state proves temporary. Peter reaches down and "raises" (ἤγειρεν) him up (v. 26), words that echo the resurrection event

---

59. Haenchen, *Acts*, 362. Martin Dibelius holds a similar position (*Studies*, 122).
60. Esler, *Community and Gospel in Luke-Acts*, 96.

wherein God "raises" (ἤγειρεν) Jesus from the dead.[61] Moreover, Peter initiates the symbolic resurrection with the command for Cornelius to "arise" (ἀνάστηθι), a command often issued to dead people prior to their return to life.[62]

In the sermon that follows, Peter explains the essential character of Jesus, the prophesied Messiah. Even though Jesus's opponents "put him to death by hanging him on a cross, God raised [ἤγειρεν] him up on the third day" (vv. 39–40). In the next breath, Peter again emphasizes the fact that Jesus "arose from the dead" (v. 41). Only through belief in Jesus as the crucified-and-risen Messiah can a person receive the "forgiveness of sins" (v. 43).

At this crucial point in Peter's sermon, the coming of the Holy Spirit on Cornelius provides the audible proof of his belief and creates solidarity between him and Jesus. The Spirit in Acts bears an exceptionally close relationship with the actual character of Jesus. In Polhill's words, "The Spirit is the abiding presence of Jesus; the Holy Spirit *is* the Spirit of Jesus (cf. 'Holy Spirit' and 'Spirit of Jesus' in 16:6–7)."[63] Thus, when Cornelius receives the Holy Spirit, he participates in a mystical union with Jesus himself.

Baptism then serves as the ritual demarcation of this intimate relationship between Cornelius and his savior. As is customary in Acts, Cornelius is baptized "in the name of Jesus Christ" (v. 48), a phrase indicative of more than a simple liturgical formula. As David Williams elaborates, the cultural importance of the name cannot be easily overlooked. Specifically, the name of Jesus "signifies his person, his power, and in a sense, his presence."[64] At the very least, Jesus's name entails the essence of his character. In one of the most comprehensive treatments of baptism in the New Testament, George Beasley-Murray offers further elaboration of the meaning of baptism in Jesus's name in Acts:

---

61. As mentioned above (n. 37), the narrator and protagonists typically rely on ἤγειρεν to describe the resurrection of Jesus. Of particular importance here, Peter soon applies the same expression to Jesus (10:40).

62. Peter uses the same command for Tabitha (9:40); Jesus does the same for Jairus's daughter (Luke 8:54; cf. 7:14). See also Conzelmann's conclusion (n. 12 above) that ἀνίστημι is often closely associated with resurrection events.

63. Polhill, *Acts*, 64.

64. Williams, *Acts*, 57.

> [T]he name of the Lord is called over the baptized, declaring him [sic] to be the Lord's, and the name is confessed and invoked by the baptized. It is this confessed relationship with the crucified, Risen Redeemer that is constitutive for Christian baptism and decisive for its significance.[65]

Hence, by baptizing in the name of Jesus, Peter ritually confirms the bond between Cornelius and the crucified-and-risen Messiah.

The conversion scene as a whole therefore clearly demonstrates the centrality of the messianic pattern. Those who become members of "The Way" must, like Cornelius, become closely united with their prospective savior, accepting him as the one who suffered on the cross and rose from the dead. Though the scene lacks a detailed replication of the messianic pattern, the narrator does preface the scene with a brief mimetic death-resurrection sequence, foreshadowing Cornelius's actual conversion through belief in and union with Jesus. In particular, the Cornelius episode verifies the truth behind the accusation against Saul; that is, when he persecutes the members of the Christian community, he persecutes Jesus himself (9:4).

CONCLUSION

Thus some of the minor characters play a significant role in the development of the motif by contributing to its efficacy. The fact that some background characters reinforce the death-resurrection message through their actions demonstrates, first of all, that the motif is present among the two different types of characters, major and minor. In this manner, the message achieves pervasiveness, necessary for a successful motif as defined by Freedman.[66]

The presence of the motif among the minor characters also means readers receive more frequent exposure to the motif. According to Freedman, "the greater the frequency with which instances of a motif recur, the deeper the impression it is likely to make on the reader."[67] Thus, the stories of Tabitha, Eutychus, the paralytics, and at least one "convert" offer persistent reminders of the death-resurrection message.

---

65. Beasley-Murray, *Baptism in the New Testament*, 120.
66. Freedman, "Literary Motif," 125.
67. Ibid., 126.

The healings of the paralytics increase the efficacy of the motif in another dimension as well. Their experiences, unlike those of Tabitha and Eutychus, show how the motif surfaces in unlikely places. Because Tabitha and Eutychus actually die and come back to life, the comparison with Jesus's experience flows naturally. The narrator must take greater pains, however, to portray the paralytic episodes as replications of the messianic pattern. By shaping their experiences in this way, the motif becomes more compelling and simultaneously satisfies Freedman's criteria of avoidability: "Clearly the more uncommon a reference in a given context, the more likely it is to strike the reader, consciously or subconsciously, and the greater will be its effect."[68]

Moreover, the strategic placement of some of these experiences within the narrative testifies to the importance of the motif.[69] The temple beggar episode becomes the first healing miracle and occurs in Jerusalem, the geographical starting point of the Christian mission to the world (1:8). Cornelius meanwhile represents the crossing of a major cultural barrier through the full acceptance of Gentiles into the Christian fold. The Eutychus story emerges at the end of Paul's public ministry. While the scenes involving the other minor characters do not occur in unimportant contexts, the healing of the temple beggar, Cornelius's conversion, and Eutychus's recovery highlight the motif through their presence at these critical junctures in the narrative.

Finally, all of the minor characters discussed in this chapter reflect a convergence of their experiences with the basic proclamation of Jesus's death and resurrection. The narrator successfully blends mimesis with diegesis to create a uniform, coherent message. The most pertinent cases, however, are the healing of the temple beggar and Cornelius's conversion; their mimetic changes revolve around the diegetic exposition of Jesus's basic character. By weaving the "showing" and the "telling" into a single stronger whole, the narrator again actualizes one of Freedman's criteria for an effective motif, the creating of a "recognizable and coherent unit."[70] The cumulative impact of the minor characters therefore serves to enrich the quality and efficacy of the motif.

---

68. Ibid.

69. An occurrence of the motif at climactic points or in significant contexts of the narrative is another of Freedman's criteria for an effective motif (ibid.).

70. Ibid., 127.

4

Intensification through Contrast: The Secondary Motif of Death and Decay

The previous chapters have argued for the pervasiveness of the death-resurrection motif. The diegetic remarks establish the motif while many of the characters reinforce it as they undergo death-resurrection types of experiences. Yet the messianic pattern becomes more striking when contrasted with a less visible yet persistent motif running concurrently through Acts, that of death and decay.

As with the former motif, this secondary one develops through diegesis (telling) and mimesis (showing). Peter and Paul, in their first extensive speeches, outline the pattern of death and decay when they contrast it with Jesus's death and resurrection. The patterns are in opposition to one another as are certain minor characters with Jesus and his followers. Those who choose to struggle against God by fighting against the people of God run the risk of reaping the fatal consequences of death and decay.

Before fleshing out the specific development of the secondary motif, however, it will be necessary to document the use of contrast as a narrative technique, revealing the plausibility of its usage in the Lukan writings. The way in which contrast functions in other texts will also inform a better understanding of its function within the Acts narrative.

WIDESPREAD USE OF CONTRAST

As in modern literature, contrast is a prominent fixture of ancient Mediterranean texts. Though most of the comments in this section will be limited to biblical materials, the use of contrast plays a major role in non-canonical works contemporary with the writing of Acts. Joze Krasovec in his study of antithetical structures notes the popularity of contrast in literature outside the Hebrew Scriptures: "In that vast literary realm [of Greek and Latin texts], both the antithesis of thought and the antithesis of form is unusually widespread. It is striking that here . . . the antithesis appears more often in prose than in poetry."[1] He then speculates that much of the early Christian literature drew on this narrative technique because of its popularity in the surrounding literary traditions.[2]

Within the biblical corpus, the importance of contrast becomes readily evident. Antithetic parallelism has long been noted as an integral part of Hebrew poetry, especially common in the Psalms and Proverbs.[3] These antitheses go beyond mere sentence structures to include contrasting images, characters, and themes.[4] Psalm 1, for example, sets forth two divergent ways of living, each with its inherent consequences: the righteous delight in the law of the Lord and will therefore prosper; in contrast, the wicked are not so and as a result will perish.[5] Not only are two lifestyles contrasted, so also are two different, albeit generalized characters, the righteous and the wicked.

Other parts of Scripture present similar poignant examples within the prose literature where one character or theme (or a combination of the two) is contrasted with another. Saul is contrasted with a ruthless

---

1. Krasovec, *Antithetic Structure*, 11.

2. Ibid., 13–14.

3. Robert Lowth first voiced the notion of "antithetic parallelism" in Lecture XIX of his *Lectures on the Sacred Poetry of the Hebrews*, first published in 1753. Cf. Westermann, *Living Psalms*, 16–17.

4. Krasovec, *Antithetic Structure*, 15. In the Hebrew Bible, the focus of his work, he notes among many others the contrast between Sisera's mother and Jael in the Song of Deborah (32–34) and the contrasting themes in the book of Job (119–23).

5. The contrast is quite evident and emphasized by commentators. Artur Weiser makes this clear with the title he gives to Psalm 1, "The Two Ways," noting the "sharp contrast" between the two lifestyles (*Psalms*, 102–8). The didactic sayings of Proverbs convey a similar message by contrasting the wise person with the foolish. Proverbs 10:5, for example, observes that "a child who gathers in summer is prudent, but a child who sleeps in harvest brings shame."

Levite,[6] Absalom with David and Joab,[7] Naaman with Gehazi,[8] Jesus with Adam,[9] hubris with humility,[10] blindness with sight,[11] gateways to life with those of destruction,[12] etc. Indeed the popularity of this technique makes it difficult to find any canonical work in which contrast does not play at least a minor role.

Within Luke's writings a variety of contrasts make their presence known. The narrator draws a distinction between Jesus and the religious authorities,[13] the rich and the poor,[14] Peter and Herod,[15] God and Satan,[16] the temple and the household,[17] light and darkness,[18] etc. Of particular importance for the present study is the contrast made in Acts between two different motifs: that of death and resurrection over against the secondary motif of death and decay. As with Psalm 1, two different ways form a contrast with one another, given support by characters within the writing. Unlike the psalm, which describes its characters in generalized terms, the narrator in Acts points to specific characters who follow one pattern or the other.

---

6. See Stuart Lasine, "Guest and Host," 37–59.

7. See Roy Battenhouse, "Tragedy of Absalom," 53–57.

8. See Robert L. Cohn, "Form and Perspective," 171–84.

9. Paul makes this basic point in Romans 5:14–21, leaving scholars with the task of defining the nuances of the contrast. James D. G. Dunn gladly obliges by devoting thirty pages of his commentary to this particular passage (*Romans 1–8*, 270–300).

10. See Willem S. Prinsloo, "Isaiah 14:12–15," 432–38. Cf. Phil 2:5–11.

11. Cf. John 9:1–41. R. Alan Culpepper, for example, notes here: "Jesus, who announced he was the light of the world (8:12), now gives sight to a man born to darkness. Gradually the blind man receives spiritual insight as well, and the blindness of the Pharisees is simultaneously revealed (9:39–41)" (*Anatomy*, 93).

12. Cf. Matt 7:13–14.

13. So observes Jack D. Kingsbury: "In stark contrast to Jesus, the religious authorities are stereotyped as those who 'serve the purposes not of God, but of humans.' The root character trait distinguishing them . . . is self-righteousness" (*Conflict in Luke*, 81).

14. Cf. L. T. Johnson, *Literary Function*, 132–44.

15. Garrett, "Exodus from Bondage," 670–77.

16. Garrett, *Demise of the Devil*.

17. Elliott, "Temple versus Household," 88–120.

18. Gaventa, *From Darkness*, esp. 52–95.

INTRADIEGETIC CONTRAST

While the primary motif of death and resurrection is established firmly on both the hyper- and intradiegetic levels,[19] the secondary motif of death and decay becomes evident primarily on the intradiegetic level. In particular, the initial missionary speeches by Peter and Paul present the tragic nature of the secondary motif, setting it in contrast to the death and resurrection of Jesus. Not only does the motif receive its impetus from two of the primary characters (Peter and Paul), but its placement in their initial evangelistic sermons enhances the importance of the contrast to the narrative.

Peter's Pentecost Speech: Acts 2:25-36

When Peter describes Jesus in his speeches, he consistently characterizes him as the one who has been put to death but raised up again by God.[20] In his first evangelistic sermon, Peter specifically explains that Jesus was "crucified and killed by the hands of those outside the law" but "God raised him up, having freed him from death" (2:23-24). Peter then buttresses his claim with an appeal to a Davidic psalm, making it apply prophetically to Jesus.[21] As such, Peter verifies the messianic status of Jesus by identifying him as the one who has not been "abandoned to Hades, nor did his flesh experience corruption" (vv. 27, 31). Instead Jesus has been able to experience the "ways of life" through his resurrection (v. 28).

In stark contrast, Peter confidently characterizes David as being in a state of death and decay. This patriarch has "both died and was buried, and his tomb is with us to this day" (v. 29). Peter's statement demonstrates the finality of David's death and decomposition.[22] Whereas God raised Jesus from the dead and exalted him to the right hand of God, David "did not ascend into heaven" (v. 34). His body remains in the tomb suffering from the natural effects of decay.

In this manner, Peter lays the two motifs side by side so that readers may understand the difference between the two. Both incorporate the

---

19. See the analysis of both types of diegetic comments in chapter 1.

20. See the analysis of Peter's speeches in chapter 1.

21. Polhill, *Acts*, 113: "Originally the psalm [Ps. 16:8-11] seems to have been a plea of the psalmist that God would vindicate him and that he might escape death and Sheol."

22. Haenchen, *Acts*, 182.

Intensification through Contrast: The Secondary Motif of Death and Decay 83

reality of death but then take diverging pathways. The primary motif reflects a cycle of death and resurrection, the other of death and decay. The former way leads to life, the latter emphasizes the consequences of death. Thus Peter magnifies the superiority of Jesus over David, along with the obvious attraction of following the pattern of Jesus over against that of death, concomitant with putrefaction.

Paul's Pisidian Antioch Speech: Acts 13:16-41, 46-47[23]

The contrast becomes more perspicuous with Paul's first major speech. God may "raise up" (ἤγειρεν) David as a temporary king (v. 22), but much more importantly, the divine hand of God "raises up" (ἤγειρεν) Jesus from the dead (v. 30).[24] God's permanent raising of Jesus makes it possible for him "no more to return to corruption" (v. 34). In so doing, God fulfills the prophecy that the Messiah will not undergo decay (v. 35). David, however, "died, was laid beside his ancestors, and experienced corruption" (v. 36). Thus the point Peter makes by inference Paul now states explicitly: David has definitely experienced the corrosive effects of decomposition (διαφθορά). Jesus is the one "whom God [truly] raised" and therefore "experienced no corruption" (v. 37). Paul's forthright approach and his repetition make the contrast unmistakably clear.[25]

In the verses that follow, Paul expounds on the practical application of the contrast. Those who accept the gospel message receive forgiveness and eternal life (vv. 38, 47-48). Those who scoff and repudiate the word of salvation will "perish" (ἀφανίσθητε) because they judge themselves "unworthy of eternal life" (vv. 41, 46). The denial of eternal life implies, through negation, that these people will be subject to the consequences of death. Moreover, by using the verb ἀφανίζω, Paul emphasizes the corrosiveness of their fatal predicament. The quote itself comes from Habakkuk 1:5, which depicts the destruction of the Israelites as they stand in judg-

---

23. I have included verses 46-47 with the speech even though these words of Paul are spoken on the following day. Paul does, however, make these comments in the same setting and links them with his previous speech as he continues to explain the consequences of repudiating the gospel.

24. Robert F. O'Toole rightly understands that these two words, in this instance, are being played off each other to heighten the contrast ("Christ's Resurrection," 367-68).

25. Noting the redundancy, Haenchen comments, "Jesus' imperishable resurrection life is contrasted once again with the transitory life of David. This gives Jesus his significance ..." which receives further explanation in the following verses (*Acts*, 412).

ment before God. In the New Testament, ἀφανίζω describes the corrosive effects of moth and rust on earthly treasures.[26]

The acceptance of or opposition to the gospel message has inherent consequences, highlighting the difference between the two opposing patterns: death and resurrection, or death and decay. Both Peter and Paul, though they regard David with esteem, find that the pattern of his death and decomposition contrasts dramatically with that of Jesus.[27] David does not oppose God, nor does his life connect with the enemies of God, but in his death, at least temporarily, David does form a contrast with Jesus. In the book of Acts, those who turn against Jesus tend to follow a path of destruction—death and decay—which is the precise description of David's present state according to the major speeches of Peter and Paul.

MIMETIC CONTRAST

What these initiatory speeches establish on the diegetic level, the characters portray on a mimetic level. The two previous chapters have shown how those who accept the message about Jesus and become his disciples tend to follow the pattern of death and resurrection. This chapter demonstrates that those who reject Jesus as the crucified-and-risen Messiah and/or turn against his followers become enemies of God and thereby subject themselves to the consequences of death and decay.

To be sure, the narrator does not describe these deadly effects for every opponent of God, but a significant sampling exists to reveal a causal link. This section examines several of these characters, beginning first with Herod Agrippa because the narrator starkly contrasts his pattern of death and decay to Peter's movement from symbolic death to renewed life. Viewing the two patterns in such close proximity to one another magnifies the distinctions and easily identifies the template of death and decay as it touches other characters in the narrative.

---

26. Cf. Matt 6:19–20.

27. The question must inevitably arise as to David's role in the pattern. David himself is not depicted by Peter and Paul as an enemy of God. Rather he is a patriarch and prophet (cf. Fitzmyer, "David," 332–39). Thus David is only connected tangentially to those who oppose God in that his death and decay forms a deadly template to be followed by those who struggle against God.

Intensification through Contrast: The Secondary Motif of Death and Decay   85

Herod Agrippa: Acts 12:20–23

Contrary to David Williams's position that the demise of Herod is a mere historical footnote "adding nothing to the main thrust of the narrative,"[28] its inclusion is vital to the story and critical for the development of the contrasting motif. In the twelfth chapter of Acts the narrator brings Peter and Herod Agrippa together in order to juxtapose the radically different pathways of each. Both confront the reality of death, but one moves from death to renewed life while the other suffers decay.

The two characters clash with one another in dramatic fashion as Herod becomes intimately involved with the persecution of Peter.[29] Herod is the one who personally arrests Peter (12:3), "seizing him and putting him in prison and delivering him to four squads of soldiers" (v. 4). Herod is also the one who intends "to bring Peter forward" before the people for judgment (vv. 4, 6). On the appointed day, Herod himself searches for Peter without success (v. 19). The narrator limns King Herod—unlike the reluctant Pilate—as actively, eagerly, and directly involved with Peter's persecution. While kings regularly give orders to their subordinates to carry out specified tasks, Herod acts without the benefit of a liaison when Peter becomes the object of his evil intentions.[30]

The whole chapter presents a struggle between a leader of the church and a leader of its opposition. Herod persecutes the church and, like Saul, finds himself in the undesirable position of opposing God.[31] The antithetic parallel between the two characters is highlighted by an angel of the Lord "striking" each character.[32] The Greek verb πατάσσω, used in both cases, shows how God rewards the followers of Jesus while simultane-

---

28. Williams, *Acts*, 5:217.

29. Garrett asserts that the portrayal of these two conflicting leaders acquires the epic proportions of the exodus with its conflict between Moses and Pharaoh and, even greater, between Jesus and Satan ("Exodus," 675–76).

30. Indeed Herod gives such orders for the execution of the guards who failed to keep Peter in prison (12:19), but he insists on direct involvement when his attention turns to Peter.

31. Saul discovers that he, by extension, persecutes Jesus whenever he oppresses the followers of Jesus (9:4–5).

32. Richard I. Pervo makes this same point: the angel wakes Peter "with a kick in the side" and then Herod later has "his turn for a kick from an angel." For the one, it brings life; for the other, it becomes "an instrument of punishment" which brings death (*Luke's Story*, 42–43).

ously punishing his opponents. The angel of the Lord "strikes" (πατάξας) Peter to awaken him from his symbolic death (12:7). The same angel then visits Herod and "strikes" (ἐπάταξεν) him so that this royal opponent is "eaten by worms and dies" (12:23).

The larger narrative contexts provide ample warning for those who wage war against God through the persecution of God's people. The Lord or the angel of the Lord periodically strikes down those who oppose God's people. When the Assyrians lay a siege to Jerusalem, an angel of the Lord "strikes" (ἐπάταξεν) the enemy's camp, leaving 185,000 dead (2 Kings 19:35). The Lord also slays individuals like Nabal who rebel against God's servant David (1 Sam 25:38). Similarly, when Jeroboam prepares to mount an attack on the people of the Southern Kingdom, Abijah, king of Judah, warns him not to "fight against the Lord God of our fathers" (2 Chr 13:12). Because the warning goes unheeded, the Lord "strikes" (ἐπάταξεν) Jeroboam during the heat of battle and again later so that he dies (2 Chr 13:15, 20). Antiochus Epiphanes likewise suffers a similar fate because he persecutes the Jewish people.[33]

Within the Acts narrative, Gamaliel issues warning to would-be persecutors of this new people of God. He advises that if the Christian movement is of God, "you will not be able to overthrow them—in that case you may even be found fighting against God!" (5:39).[34] Waging such a war, as many Judeo-Christian texts make clear, is an effort in futility with deadly consequences: "Woe to the nations that rise up against my people! The Lord Almighty will take vengeance on them in the day of judgment; he will send fire and worms into their flesh; they shall weep in pain forever" (Jdt 16:17).[35] Herod refuses to heed the warning and consequently suffers a mortal blow from his own confrontation with the Lord.[36]

---

33. Ὁ δὲ πανεπόπτης Κύριος ὁ θεός τοῦ Ἰσραὴλ ἐπάταξεν αὐτὸν ἀνιάτῳ καὶ ἀοράτῳ πληγῇ (2 Macc 9:5).

34. The narrator here uses Gamaliel as a foil in order to present syllogistic reasoning in support of the Christian movement. Gamaliel lays the framework for two related syllogisms born out in the narrative. First, if this plan (βουλή) belongs to God, it cannot be overthrown. This plan cannot be overthrown. Therefore, it must belong to God. Second, fighting against God's plan is the same as fighting against God. Christians are part of God's plan. Therefore, fighting against Christians is the same as fighting against God.

35. This theme is especially common among writings penned during times of persecution. Cf. Isa 14, Ezek 27–28; Rev 13, 17.

36. Conzelmann rightly concludes that Herod's death is "due not only to his hubris, but to his role as persecutor" (*Acts*, 96).

Intensification through Contrast: The Secondary Motif of Death and Decay   87

The narrator's description of him as "eaten by worms" (σκωληκόβρωτος) signifies both the painfulness of his death and the physical decay of his body. As Hans Conzelmann claims, "To be eaten by worms (or by lice) is the typical death for one who despises God."[37] Those who persecute God's people run a particularly high risk of this punishment. After the Lord strikes Antiochus Epiphanes, an ardent enemy of the Jewish people, his body "swarms with worms, and . . . his flesh rots away, and because of the stench the whole army feels revulsion at his decay" (2 Macc 9:9). Herod the Great, another tyrannical persecutor, suffered a similar fate. Josephus recounts in the story of his death that acute abdominal pains and rot-producing worms severely afflicted Herod in his dying days.[38] In both cases, the writers emphasize the painfulness of their deaths as a divine recompense for the wickedness of their reigns, reaping the corrosive effects of death before they reach their burial plots.[39]

While the presence of worms intensifies the painfulness of death, these wriggling flesh eaters also provide vivid evidence of death's rot and decay. The book of Sirach, for example, expresses proverbially how the dead inherit "maggots, beasts, and worms" (10:11; cf. 19:3).[40] Job likewise connects decay with worms by using the phrase "in the corruption of worms" (ἐν σαπρίᾳ σκωλήκων), demonstrating the close relationship between the two concepts.[41] At times, the two terms become synonymous. The Septuagint, for example, uses σαπρία in Job 17:14 and 21:26, while the Hebrew equivalent relies simply on the word for worm, *rimah*, to describe the process of decomposition associated with death. Not surprisingly, Norman C. Habel notes in his commentary on Job that worms are typically associated with death and often become "the mark of one decimated by decay."[42]

---

37. Ibid., 96–97. Cf. Herodotus *Persian Wars* 4:205; Pausanius 9.7.2–3; Pliny the Elder *Natural History* 7:172; Lucian of Samosata *Alexander the False Prophet* 59; Mark 9:47–48.

38. More specifically, Herod was afflicted by "an ulceration of the bowels and intestinal pains that were particularly terrible. . . . And he suffered similarly from an abdominal ailment, as well as from a gangrene of his privy parts that produced worms" (Josephus *Ant.* 17:169).

39. Ibid. 17:168; 2 Macc 9:6.

40. Worms also cause the decay or spoilage of plants and food (Exod 16:20; Deut 28:39; Prov 12:4; 25:20).

41. E.g., Job 2:9; 7:5; cf. 2 Macc 9:9.

42. Habel, *Book of Job*, 279. One of the definitions for *rimah* is "cause and sign of decay" (BDB, 942).

Herod Agrippa therefore functions as a striking example of one who follows the pattern of death and decay as the result of his opposition to God's people. The narrator draws an intimate connection between him and Peter to demonstrate the dramatic contrast between the pair. Peter follows the pattern of death and resurrection, Herod the pathway of death and decay.

Judas: Acts 1:16–20

As the Herod incident testifies, fighting against God has deadly consequences. Though Herod's demise may leave the deepest impression on readers, he does not descend into the depths by himself. Among those who belong to the same group, Judas is the precursor. He also precedes the explanations about death and decay, and as such his death can be fully understood only as the narrative progresses. Nevertheless, his turning against Jesus results in his own demise. While the suffering and death of Jesus together with his resurrection brings salvation to those who respond positively, the memorial to Judas's death is a note about his rotting corpse left in a state of decay.

Judas, like Jesus, fulfills a prophetic imperative from the Scriptures. Unlike Jesus, Judas serves the negative role of being an enemy of God's chosen one. "It is necessary" (δεῖ) for Judas to play the role of Jesus's betrayer, as "the Holy Spirit foretold by the mouth of David" (1:16). The extended contexts of the psalms quoted in verse 20 refer to enemies of God's anointed one.[43] For this reason, both Conzelmann and F. F. Bruce suggest that Luke paints Judas as an enemy of God who receives his just recompense for his opposition to God's appointed servant.[44] Moreover,

---

43. Although the identity of the precise psalms remains uncertain, the most likely candidates are Psalms 69 and 109. Both refer to enemies who persecute God's anointed one.

44. Conzelmann, *Acts*, 11. F. F. Bruce explains the process in this way: "[I]n light of Jesus' passion, many of the afflictions endured by a righteous sufferer in the Psalms were also interpreted of him. It followed that what was said of the enemies of the Lord's anointed or of the righteous sufferer would be interpreted of the enemies of Jesus (cf. 4:25–28). Among his enemies, Judas was unenviably prominent, and it was not difficult to find Old Testament texts which pointed to him" (*Book of Acts*, 45). For a detailed analysis of this topic, see Wilhelm Nestle's dated but useful article, "Legenden vom Tod," 246–69.

Intensification through Contrast: The Secondary Motif of Death and Decay

Peter characterizes Judas as the "guide to those who arrested Jesus" (1:16), the role of an enemy and instrument of Satan.[45]

Because Judas assumes this unenviable role, he must face the deadly consequences of his choice. The narrator whispers the details of his death in an aside, a version that incidentally has created not a few hermeneutical problems.[46] John Polhill offers perhaps the best literal reading of the Greek: "And becoming prone, he burst in the middle, and all his entrails poured out" (1:18).[47] The ambiguity of first phrase, "becoming prone" (πρηνὴς γενόμενος), has posed challenges for both early and contemporary interpreters. The phrase is usually translated problematically as "falling headlong." A variant reading ameliorates the difficulty by replacing πρηνής with πρησθείς.[48] The most likely reading, however, is πρηνής. The same word is used in the Book of Wisdom to describe the destruction of the ungodly who afflict the righteous:

> For [the Lord] shall rend them and cast them down headlong, that they shall be speechless [ὅτι ῥήξει αὐτοὺς ἀφώνους πρηνεῖς]; and he shall shake them from the foundation; and they shall be utterly laid waste, and be in sorrow; and their memorial shall perish. (4:19)

The context in Acts, like that of the Book of Wisdom, is one of judgment, making πρηνής an appropriate choice for the narrator's description of Judas.

In contrast to the Matthean account, Luke Timothy Johnson demonstrates that the Luke-Acts narratives clearly depict Judas as a permanent defector deserving judgment: Judas's "buying a farm for himself is the exact opposite of the way the believers in 4:32ff sold their farms and fields to share possessions with all" and of the disciples' leaving everything to

---

45. Mikeal Parsons aptly notes the similarities and contrasts between Peter and Judas ("Christian Origins," 405). They both fulfill Jesus's prophecy; for one betrayal, and the other denial. Yet the contrast arises because "Satan entered Judas" (Luke 22:3), but Peter receives the opportunity to turn again to the faith (22:31–32).

46. The story differs from the account given in Matthew, and the language is vague and complicated by variant readings.

47. Polhill, *Acts*, 92.

48. The variant πρησθείς, meaning "to swell," likely derives from Papias's version that the body of Judas swelled to enormous proportions so that he was unable to pass through an area large enough for a horse and cart.

follow Jesus (Luke 5:11).[49] Johnson therefore concludes that Judas's purchase of the farm is "a symbol of his apostasy from the community of the Twelve."[50] According to Parsons, naming that place the "Field of Blood" further verifies that Judas dies under the judgment of God, with his property "doomed to perpetual desertion."[51]

Other enemies of God similarly take literal falls leading to their deaths. Jezebel, with the help of her eunuchs, falls from a window to her death (2 Kgs 9:32-33). Antiochus Epiphanes takes a hard fall from his chariot, eventually causing his death.[52] Josephus describes the death of an aggressive Roman soldier named Sabinus, who, after stumbling over a rock, "falls headlong" (πρηνὴς ... κατέπεσεν) with the result that a group of nearby Jews are able to kill him.[53]

Whether Judas stumbles over a rock or falls from a rooftop matters little.[54] The narrator's primary emphasis becomes clear: Judas, as an enemy of God's people, receives his just punishment. Πρηνής fits this purpose well because the word seems to be commonly associated with judgment of God's enemies, concomitant with their destruction.[55]

The latter part of the narrator's aside further confirms Judas's total destruction and decay as an enemy of God's people. When Judas "burst open in the middle" so that "all his entrails pour out" (ἐξεχύθη πάντα τὰ σπλάγχνα αὐτοῦ), his painful death becomes certain. The Septuagint records a similar incident about Amasa, whose "entrails pour out on the ground" (ἐξεχύθη ἡ κοιλία αὐτοῦ εἰς τήν γῆν). Because his death is thereby evident, Joab finds it unnecessary to stab him a second time (2

---

49. Johnson, *Literary Function*, 180.

50. Ibid.

51. Parsons, "Christian Origins," 406.

52. Cf. 2 Macc 9:7-28. Josephus notes that Antiochus falls from his chariot with a description similar to the narrator's description of Judas. Josephus uses κατὰ γῆν γενόμενος (2 Macc 9:8) while the narrative aside in Acts has πρηνὴς γενόμενος (1:18).

53. *War* 6:64.

54. Haenchen adopts the position that Judas fell headlong from the rooftop of his house (*Acts*, 160). Conzelmann suggests the further possibility of Judas falling from a cliff (*Acts*, 11).

55. Πρηνής also commonly refers to a description of someone in a prostrate position (cf. Josephus *Ant.* 18:59; *War* 1:621; Posidonius 57, frag. 5). The narrator may therefore also be indicating that God has thoroughly humbled Judas in his death (cf. Isa 14 where God abases the Babylonian king).

Intensification through Contrast: The Secondary Motif of Death and Decay 91

Sam 20:10).⁵⁶ Catullus, a vicious enemy of the Jews, also dies after losing his entrails, strongly warning other potential enemies:

> His malady ever growing rapidly worse, his bowels ulcerated and fell out [τῶν ἐντέρων αὐτῷ κατὰ διάβρωσιν ἐκπεσόντων]; and so he died, affording a demonstration, no less striking than any, how God in his providence inflicts punishment on the wicked.⁵⁷

Thus, the description of a person's bowels being afflicted and falling out was not an uncommon way to describe the painfulness and certainty of death, often reflecting the judgment of God.

As the one who betrays Jesus, Judas becomes a type of antiChrist. He not only turns against Jesus, but he also models the consequences of those who will later fight against God by persecuting the Messiah's followers. While Jesus moves from an undeserved death to resurrected life, Judas moves from a punitive death to decay. The opening scenes of Acts demonstrates that Jesus's body does not decay but rather returns from the dead and ascends into heaven; however, the narrative leaves the corpse of Judas splattered across the ground rotting in the open air. In short, Jesus inherits eternal life, Judas a "field of blood."

Ananias and Sapphira: Acts 5:1–11

Although the decaying body of Judas at the territorial borders of the narrative warns others who enter the story not to challenge God, some still refuse to heed the warning and thereby suffer similar consequences. Such is the fate of Ananias and Sapphira. Like Judas, they challenge God from within the community of believers. Like Judas, they suffer death and decay.

---

56. Cf. Judg 3:12–25. Here Ehud delivers the Israelites from Moabite oppression by killing Eglon, the king of Moab. Ehud, like Joab, stabs his victim in the belly (κοιλία), resulting in his death. Two *hapax logomena* make the full description of Eglon's death and Ehud's escape ambiguous (3:22–23). The LXX leaves the first *hapax* untranslated, but the Targum and the Vulgate both translate it as "the excrement poured out." This is also the translation adopted by Rabbi Avrohom Fishelis and Rabbi Shmuel Fishelis in their authoritative commentary on Judges (*Judges*, 24). Such a reading proves appropriate, making use of Hebrew pun and irony: When the excrement "comes out," Ehud can "go out," his job having been completed. The delay of Eglon's return from his chamber prompts his servants to believe that he is "relieving himself" (3:24). Ironically, they find their hypothesis to be correct only not in the manner they expected.

57. *War* 7:453.

The Ananias and Sapphira episode echoes the story of Achan, who lived during the time of ancient Israelite conquest.[58] Not only do both cases involve a compromise of the community through the concealment of property, but both episodes also end with capital punishment for the guilty person's family members. The Acts narrator solidifies the allusion to the Achan episode through the description of their crimes. Both have "embezzled" property resulting in harmful effects on the life of the community.[59] Ananias, with his wife's knowledge, "kept back" (ἐνοσφίσατο) part of the money for himself (5:2) just as Achan had "kept back" (ἐνοσφίσαντο) some of the forbidden spoils of battle (Josh 7:1, 20–21).

Because of their sin, they must suffer the consequences of death. Though the punishment for Ananias and Sapphira seems unduly severe,[60] their sin is particularly grievous due to their lying to (5:3) and testing of (5:9) the Holy Spirit, thereby harming the community. The group of Jerusalem believers, who had been "filled with the Holy Spirit" (4:31) and "of one heart" (4:32), is now a divided community because Ananias's heart has been filled by God's archenemy Satan (5:3). Peter restores the Christian community by pronouncing God's fatal judgment on them (vv. 9, 12).[61]

The terminology used to describe the death of this couple also points to God's judgment. The narrator, when depicting their death, uses ἐκψύχω in both cases (vv. 5, 10). Haenchen rightly confirms that this rare term "is applied to the death of one struck by divine punishment."[62] Herod dies (ἐξέψυξεν) in the same way after being struck by the angel of the Lord (12:23). The Septuagint reserves this verb to describe the death of Sisera

---

58. Although the parallels with the Achan episode are strong, other possibilities also exist. Daniel Marguerat finds powerful allusions to the original sin in the Garden of Eden which similarly involves deception and disrupts life of the community ("Mort D'Ananias et Saphira," 222–25).

59. In Achan's case, the ancient Israelites fell in defeat before the small city of Ai (Josh 7:2–5). In Acts, the deceit of Ananias and Sapphira compromise the unity of the Christian community (cf. Polhill, *Acts*, 156).

60. Polhill's observation: "The judgment on these two seems so harsh, so nonredemptive, so out of keeping with the gospel" (*Acts*, 155); cf. Marshall, *Acts*, 110.

61. Haenchen points out that "Peter's declaration, introduced by ἰδού is not a prophecy... but a pronouncement of the divine judgment and its immediate execution" (*Acts*, 239).

62. Ibid., 238.

(Judg 4:21 [Codex Alexandrinus]) and the fatal plight of Israel in Ezekiel's prophecies of doom (Ezek 21:7).

The burial of Ananias and Sapphira confirms their fate. After each one dies, the young men of the Christian community arrive to carry out the burial procedures (vv. 6, 10), echoing the pattern of David's death and burial (2:29). Like David, their bodies will be subject to decomposition (13:36). While scholars may debate the possibility of future restoration for the pair,[63] the narrative leaves them in the grave. Their fate is death followed by decay because they die as enemies of God/God's people.[64]

The Death and Decay of the Devil

In her well-received work *The Demise of the Devil*, Susan Garrett argues that the defeat of Satan's earthly agents in Luke's writings provides evidence for the decline and ultimate demise of Satan himself.[65] The Lukan narratives continually portray the destruction of one evil agent after the other. In fact all of the characters mentioned in this chapter may justifiably be categorized as servants of Satan who fall into death and decay.[66] Because of their especially close connection with Satan, however, discussion of Simon Magus and Elymas has been reserved for this last section to show

---

63. Munck claims that the pair have no hope because they have committed the "unforgivable sin" (Munck, *Acts*, 41); Polhill, however, believes that their punishment does not "necessarily involve their loss of salvation" (Polhill, *Acts*, 161).

64. This is the key difference between Stephen and Ananias and Sapphira. Stephen's death parallels that of Jesus through his innocence and the words he speaks. Moreover Jesus stands on Stephen's behalf. There is every reason to believe that this Christian martyr will complete the pattern of Jesus in the fulfillment of resurrected life (cf. the Stephen section in chapter 2). On the other hand, Ananias and Sapphira align themselves with Satan and die in judgment as the enemies of God. Their burials are hurried, and no tears are shed over their departure. They therefore follow the pattern of Judas, with no expectation of restoration.

65. Garrett develops the thesis throughout her work, using particular events, sayings, and confrontations with Satan's earthly agents to demonstrate his declining power while simultaneously pointing to his eventual destruction. The final victory over Satan will be fully realized in the future. Yet within the Lukan narratives, "Satan and his demonic and human servants" can no longer "harass and torment at will. Satan's kingdom [is] splintering around him, and his authority [is] no longer acknowledged by all. The battle still rages but Christ's ultimate triumph [is] certain" (*Demise of the Devil*, 108-9).

66. Indeed, Garrett does classify all of the characters of this chapter under Satan's authority, though she mentions Judas, Ananias and Sapphira, and Herod only briefly in *Demise*. For Herod's link with Satan, see her article "Exodus from Bondage," 675-77.

their downfall as particularly presaging the demise of Satan. Building on Garrett's thesis, I argue that both of these magicians fall into a deathlike state, pointing to the eventual destruction of the Devil.

Simon Magus: Acts 8:9–24

After Philip journeys to Samaria and preaches the "word" (λογος) (8:4; cf. 8:14), many people respond positively including Simon Magus who "believes, and after being baptized, continues on with Philip" (v. 13). The first part of the episode reveals that Simon has been a practitioner of magic, "regarding himself as someone great" (λέγων εἶναί τινα ἑαυτόν μέγαν) (v. 9). His role as a magician places him in opposition to God; his unabated pride sets the stage for his demise.[67] Gamaliel reports Theudas's making a similar claim for himself prior to his fall: λέγων εἶναί τινα ἑαυτόν.[68] In fact, the Western text adds μέγαν to the boast in Acts 5:36, making the two claims synonymous.

Though scholars debate the authenticity of Simon's conversion,[69] the attention of the narrative focuses on the distinction between two different amazing feats, one originating from God and the other from Satan. While Peter works miracles, Simon practices magic, which represents a challenge to the early church, whether internal or external to the com-

---

67. Both Jews and Christians often perceived magicians as agents of Satan in direct opposition to God. Cf. P. Samain, "L'Accusation de magie," 454–55. Pride, meanwhile, is one of the common denominators for Satan and his followers, leading to their demise.

68. Josephus reports about a Theudas who gathered a large group of followers together at the Jordan River, boasting that at his command "the river would be parted and would provide them an easy passage" (*Ant.* 20:97). Though the identification of this Theudas with the one mentioned in Acts 5:36 is not certain nor without its problems (cf. Bruce, *Book of Acts*, 116), such an identification fits the narrative context well because the Theudas of Josephus's *Antiquities* is said to be a γόης which becomes a fitting parallel to Simon the magician.

69. Williams believes that Simon "had not entered into the meaning of baptism and had neither truly confessed Jesus as Lord nor received his salvation" (*Acts*, 158); Stagg sees Simon as unconverted and the "core of depravity" (*Book of Acts*, 104); Polhill likewise notes that Simon "had not responded to the gospel; he had responded to greed" (*Acts*, 220). On the other hand, Haenchen understands the magician to have truly converted and subsequently fallen away though he is presented with a second opportunity contrary to the view expressed in Hebrews (*Acts*, 305); Bruce finds his faith "sincere, but superficial and inadequate" (*Book of Acts*, 167); Arnold Ehrhardt similarly understands him to be sincere albeit immature, but he places the blame on Peter for Simon's loss: "St Peter trampled down the new plantation of St Philip" (*Acts*, 47).

Intensification through Contrast: The Secondary Motif of Death and Decay 95

munity.⁷⁰ This challenge originates from within the community when the new believer Simon offers money for the authority to dispense the Holy Spirit. Peter immediately identifies such a proposition as a blasphemous desire leading Simon "into destruction" (εἰς ἀπώλειαν). The apostle therefore proclaims, "To hell with you and your silver" (v. 20).⁷¹ With this pronouncement, Simon—though he appeared to be great—is poised for destruction.

Peter heaps further condemnation upon him: "You have no part or portion in this word!" (v. 21).⁷² Such a statement again questions Simon's status. Is Peter implying that Simon has never been a member of this community or that he has now lost his previous position among God's people? Biblical scholars and grammarians remain divided on the issue.⁷³

If Simon follows the pattern of Judas, Peter's pronouncement indicates that this Samarian miscreant no longer has a place among God's people. A strong parallel exists between Judas and Simon, rendering a "fall from grace" the more plausible interpretation. Both characters succumb to greed; one desires to gain money through betrayal (Luke 22:3–6), the other by profiting from a newly acquired "trick" (Acts 8:18–19). Both cases involve ἀργύριον (Luke 5:22; Acts 8:20). In judgment, both face the loss of their portion or inheritance (κλῆρος) among God's people (Acts 1:17; 8:20; cf. 26:18). Thus Peter's harsh statement is likely more proscriptive than descriptive; that is, Simon will no longer have an inheritance among God's people.

Peter becomes descriptive when he gives the reasons behind his cursing of Simon. He looks at Simon and sees him wallowing in the "gall of bitterness and in the bondage of iniquity" (8:23), revealing Simon's woe-

---

70. Luke's narrator seems to have little concern for broaching such theological issues as "security of the believer" or the possibility of forgiveness for those who have "tasted of God's grace" and subsequently "fallen away." The cases of Judas and Ananias and Sapphira give the indication that defection of true followers from the community is certainly possible.

71. Such is the translation given by Haenchen (*Acts*, 304). Conzelmann notes that Peter's imprecation takes the form of a curse (*Acts*, 66).

72. Though some versions translate τῷ λόγῳ τούτῳ in a more generic sense such as "this matter" (nasb), "this word" corresponds with the message that Philip has been preaching (8:4, 14). The "word" signifies the message of salvation, an abbreviated way of referring to the salvific effects of the death and resurrection of Jesus (see chapter 1).

73. See the discussion above about Simon's status. The phrase οὐκ ἔστιν σοι μερὶς οὐδὲ κλῆρος allows either meaning.

ful condition. The first half of the phrase (χολὴν πικρίας) derives from Deuteronomy 29:18, in which idolaters within the Ancient Israelite community face severe condemnation.[74] The Lord will "blot out their names from under heaven" (Deut 29:20). They will "utterly perish" (ἀπωλείᾳ ἀπολεῖσθε) and lose their inheritance (Deut 30:18; cf. Acts 8:20–21).

Peter also envisions Simon as a prisoner held captive by the "chains of iniquity" (σύνδεσμον ἀδικίας, 8:23). Jesus came to set such prisoners free (Luke 4:18), but Simon has chosen to go back into captivity.[75] As a prisoner, he has moved into the realm of symbolic death. He does not follow the pattern of Jesus who broke free from the fetters of death (Acts 2:24).[76] Instead Simon chooses to follow the way of death and destruction.

Though Peter gives Simon the chance to repent, Simon remains in a passive deathlike state, unable or unwilling to make his own cry for repentance.[77] Garrett aptly compares his request for Peter's intercession with that of Pharaoh's desire for Moses to intercede on behalf of the Egyptians.[78] The implication: Simon, like Pharaoh, is not truly repentant; he is merely seeking to avoid further harm. Both hearts remain hardened.

The Western text adds a detail—Simon's profuse weeping—to the scene (8:24). Even if accepted as part of the narrative, however, these tears do not necessarily demonstrate his repentance. Within the Luke-Acts narratives, weeping is a sign of "personal distress or sorrow rather than repentance."[79] Coupled with the severity of Peter's curse and Simon's self-centered ambitions, such weeping reflects the distress arising from his deadly predicament.[80] Not coincidentally, other writings contemporary with Acts picture Satan as weeping in the face of defeat.[81]

---

74. These are the ones who make idols of silver (ἀργύριον) and gold (Deut 29:17).

75. The quote comes from Isaiah 58:6 in which the Lord desires that the "fetters of iniquity be loosened [λύε πάντα σύνδεσμον ἀδικίας]."

76. Peter conveys the image of freedom from the cords of death despite following the Septuagint's mistranslation of *chebel* as "birth pangs" instead of "fetters" (cf. Haenchen, *Acts*, 180).

77. Conzelmann notes "the powerlessness of the magician before the one who bears the Spirit" (*Acts*, 66).

78. Garrett, *Demise*, 72.

79. Ibid.

80. In Garrett's words, Simon "resembles a cornered criminal, frightened at the prospect of punishment although not obviously remorseful over his crimes" (*Demise*, 72).

81. In the Testament of Job, Satan weeps and cowers in shame after his unsuccessful attacks on Job (27:1–7).

Elymas the Magician: Acts 13:6–11

Another magician falls from power into a state of death when Paul confronts Bar Jesus (alias Elymas) in Cyprus. Unlike the challenge from Simon Magus, Elymas attacks from outside the community of believers. In both cases, however, the outcome is the same, foreshadowing the fate of their master.

The confrontation between Paul and Elymas gains importance with the implication of the forces behind each contestant. The narrator characterizes Paul as one directly commissioned by God through the Holy Spirit (13:2), a proclaimer of the word of God (v. 5), and a person "filled with the Holy Spirit (v. 9). By contrast, the narrator describes Bar Jesus as a magician and false prophet who seeks "to turn the proconsul away from the faith" (vv. 6, 8). In his speech Paul further clarifies that Bar Jesus is "full of all deceit and villainy" and an "enemy of all righteousness" who continually makes "crooked the straight paths of the Lord" (v. 10).[82] Garrett explains the sinister implications of such a characterization:

> In light of such [Jewish and Christian] eschatological traditions it seems likely that Bar Jesus' composite identity as magician, false prophet and satanic stand-in was neither fortuitous nor insignificant; these three roles were thought to belong together. . . . Indeed he had a *double* "double identity": he was Bar Jesus and also Elymas; he was magus serving the esteemed Sergius Paulus and also a false prophet serving Satan.[83]

In short, Paul and the narrator characterize him as specifically related to and controlled by the devil, and as Garrett aptly notes, "the very antithesis of the Holy Spirit."[84] Thus Paul rightly corrects the ancestry of Elymas, identifying him as a child of Satan rather than a son of Jesus.[85]

Because Elymas opposes God's work, Paul pronounces a curse on him so that the "hand of the Lord" causes a mist and a darkness to fall upon him (v. 11). Elymas loses his sight, thereby entering the domain of darkness and symbolic death. Paul also claims that this magician-false

---

82. Garrett, *Demise*, 81.

83. Ibid.

84. Ibid., 80. "Thus the confrontation between Bar Jesus and Paul is also a confrontation between the Holy Spirit and the devil."

85. More specifically, Paul addresses him as a "son of the Devil" (13:10), creating a pun with the Aramaic "bar (son of)" to emphasize his point.

prophet will "not see the sun," a common euphemism for death in Greek and Hebrew literature.[86] Job, for example, speaks of infants who die before birth as those who never "see the light" (3:16). Conversely, Euripides employs the positive version of the idiom, "to see the sun," as a circumlocution for life: "While Proteus yet saw the light of the sun [i.e., was alive], I lived unharmed" (*Helen* 60).[87] Thus, while the context of the passage in Acts requires the phrase to be translated as blindness, there persists a strong allusion to death through both the common understanding of the terminology and the symbolism.

Because of his blindness, Elymas must "grope around for someone to lead him by the hand" (v. 11).[88] His condition echoes that of the ones who reap the curses of the Mosaic covenant due to their turning against God. Deuteronomy 28:28-29 proclaims that the Lord will "afflict you with madness, blindness, and confusion of mind; you shall grope about at noon as blind people grope in darkness, but you shall be unable to find your way." Such dire helplessness, like those in Sheol, confirms Elymas's fate as one of symbolic death.

Death, moreover, is the prescribed punishment meted out to false prophets. Any prophet who "speaks in the name of other gods, or who presumes to speak in my name a word that I have not commanded the

---

86. Earl Richard's study of the phrase in Greek and Hebrew texts led him to this precise conclusion: "In Classical and Hellenistic Greek [and biblical Hebrew], 'not to see the sun' means 'to be dead,' or positively, 'to see the light' means 'to be alive'" ("Old Testament in Acts," 332). After citing two examples, Richard comments in a footnote that "similar evidence spans the whole of Greek literature from Homer to Plutarch" (ibid.). He also notes that the phrase's meaning in Hebrew is the same as it is in Greek.

87. Cf. Josephus *Ant.* 16:99, where Herod does not believe it advantageous for some of his children "to see the light of the sun [i.e., to live] after what they had planned to do."

88. Though the description of blindness shows a similarity with that of Paul's (9:8), the narrative places them in contrast, not comparison, to one another. Garrett marks out the points of contrast:

> (1) Bar Jesus is said to 'make straight paths crooked' but Paul is led to "a street called straight" (9:11); (2) Bar Jesus is blinded by mist and darkness (13:11), but Paul had been blinded by an intensely bright light (22:11; 26:13); (3) whereas Paul eventually made the transition from darkness to light, Bar Jesus' blindness is not relieved within the context of the narrative. The differences in experience signify the diverging paths or "ways" of their lives (Garrett, *Demise*, 84).

The Acts narrative therefore points out the differences between the two: Paul makes the transition from symbolic death to renewed life, but Elymas remains in a state of symbolic death and decay.

Intensification through Contrast: The Secondary Motif of Death and Decay 99

prophet to speak—that prophet shall die" (Deut 18:20; cf. 13:1–5).⁸⁹ The law finds application in the Hebrew narratives during the time of prophetic challenges.⁹⁰ Elijah challenges the many false prophets of Baal in the dramatic feat of calling fire from heaven to consume a sacrifice (1 Kgs 18). Because of the successful results of Elijah and the unsuccessful efforts of the Baal prophets, Elijah is exonerated as a true prophet of God while the others are put to death (18:40). When the prophet Jeremiah confronts his counterfeit opponents, he, like Paul, pronounces God's death sentence on them. Jeremiah condemns Hananiah by telling him the Lord will "send you off the face of the earth. Within this year you will be dead because you have spoken rebellion against the Lord" (Jer 28:16 [35:16 LXX]).⁹¹ His prophecy reaches fulfillment with the death of Hananiah in the seventh month of that year (28:17 [35:17 LXX]). Thus, in the context of prophetic challenge as the narrator of Acts sets the stage, the death of the false prophet is the logical consequence.

What about the permanence of Elymas's condition? Paul proclaims that this magician-false prophet will "not see the sun *for a time*" (ἄχρι καιροῦ) (13:11), which seems to make his blindness ephemeral, thereby failing to follow the pattern of permanent death and decay. However, in this context of judgment the phrase "for a time" likely emphasizes the "decisive (i.e., not instantly fleeting) quality" of the punishment rather than pointing to a future hope of recovery.⁹² Such curses tend to pass on permanent rather than temporary consequences.⁹³ Appropriately, the

---

89. This judgment is particularly important because of its context. Deuteronomy 18:9–14 declares a resounding condemnation of sorcerers and magicians, a cause for their dispossession. Immediately following is the passage that speaks about raising up a prophet like Moses (Deut 18:15, 18). As David Moessner argues, Luke relies heavily on these passages, incorporating their themes into the Gospel and Acts ("Paul and the Pattern," 203–12). As true prophets, Paul and his companions wage a war against the magician-false prophets.

90. As in Elijah's case, the narrator in Acts pictures Paul as facing a prophetic challenge. Paul is the true prophet while Elymas plays the undesirable role of the false prophet (cf. Tannehill, *Narraive Unity*, 2:162).

91. Jeremiah likewise condemns Ahab son of Kolaiah and Zedekiah son of Maaseiah who are prophesying lies in the name of the Lord. These are to suffer death at the hands of Nebuchadrezzar (Jer 29:21–23 [36:21–23 LXX]).

92. Garrett, *Demise*, 85. The scene represents for Garrett the resounding defeat of Satan's servant and an indication of what the future holds for Satan himself.

93. The Deuteronomy passage itself speaks of permanent deadly consequences: "The Lord will cause you to be defeated before your enemies . . . . Your corpses shall be food

narrative ends with Elymas in a state of symbolic death: blindness and helplessness (v. 11).

Implications for Satan

More importantly, the deadly defeat of Simon and Elymas depicts on a small scale what will happen to their master. Satan, like Simon, is full of pride, boasting greatness and desiring worship from all (Luke 4:5–7). Because of his unabated pride, Satan is poised for disaster. Indeed, Jesus already claims he sees Satan "falling like lightning from the sky" (Luke 10:18), thereby projecting his eschatological fall from power into death and destruction.[94] The most likely background of his prediction derives from Isaiah 14:4–20. Garrett documents the practice of intertestamental writers grafting this taunt for the king of Babylon onto Satan himself, making it a packaged concept ready to be employed by Luke's narrator.[95] In this passage, Isaiah reprimands the Babylonian king for his boastful claims and his attacks on the chosen people of God. The proud king will therefore descend into Hades (mt Sheol) where maggots (σῆψιν) will become his bed and worms (σκώληξ) his blanket (Isa 14:11).[96] By applying the taunt to Satan, Luke implies that this archenemy of God will likewise fall into destruction and make his bed in decay.

The second part of the taunt applies equally well to the message in Acts on the issue of dispossession. Isaiah 14:21–23 pronounces a curse on the children of the Babylonian king, calling for them to lose their inheritance. The children of Satan can likewise expect to lose their inheritance (κλῆρας), illustrated through Simon's loss as well as that of Judas and Ananias and Sapphira.

---

for every bird of the air and animal of the earth, and there shall be no one to frighten them away" (28:25–26).

94. Garrett, *Demise*, 40: "Given Luke's horror at the prospect of misdirected worship, Satan's arrogation of divine glory—culminating in his brazen effort to persuade even Jesus to worship him—must have drastic consequences. Accordingly, Luke 4:6–7 ought to be paired with the remark in 10:18 about Satan's fall."

95. Ibid. Cf. *L.A.E.* 12:1—16:3.

96. Isaiah 14:15, 19 further elaborate on his fate: "You will be thrust down to Sheol, to the recesses of the pit. . . . you have been cast out of your tomb like a rejected branch, clothed with the slain who are pierced with a sword, who go down to the stones of the pit" (nasb).

CONCLUSION

The secondary motif of death and decay therefore plays a significant role in the Acts narrative. Peter and Paul establish the motif on the diegetic level as they contrast the patterns of Jesus and David. While God raises Jesus from the dead, David remains in the tomb with his body being subject to decay. While David himself is highly esteemed, his temporary state of decay in contrast to Jesus provides an example of the permanent punishment that will be meted out to the enemies of the Christian community. Accordingly, Paul warns in his speech that these enemies—those who reject the message about Jesus and place themselves in opposition to God—will perish. Through their actions, they have become unworthy of eternal life. In short, they will follow the pattern of death and decay.

On the mimetic level, the characters following this sinister pattern fight against God by struggling against God's people. Judas, in his betrayal of Jesus, becomes a kind of antiChrist and a precursor to the subsequent enemies of God within the narrative. Ananias and Sapphira follow in his footsteps to death and decay, as does Herod Agrippa, all in a very literal sense. Simon Magus and Elymas follow Judas symbolically; that is, they fall into states of symbolic death through their perilous circumstances. These latter two characters in particular prefigure the eventual demise of Satan. As the source of inspiration for these enemies of God, Satan will also suffer death and decay.

The vivid contrast between the two motifs becomes evident when Herod clashes with Peter. The narrator lays the two scenes beside each other in such a way that eaders see the two patterns clearly, thereby highlighting the distinctions. The angel of the Lord "touches" Peter, lifting him from symbolic death to renewed life; the same angel "touches" Herod, throwing him into death and decay.

The contrasting motifs function in much the same way as other contrasts within the biblical literature. Some of the most important effects include clarification, intensification, and persuasion. First, contrast helps to clarify through negation: to define by saying what something is not. Though the pattern of Jesus includes suffering and death, this suffering is efficacious and followed by new life. That means the followers of Jesus do not experience perpetual suffering or everlasting decay. Eternal death and decomposition become an inheritance for the enemies of God.

Second, the narrator intensifies the message of the story by juxtaposing the antithetical positions. The benefits of following "The Way" become more desirable when contrasted with the judgment meted out to those who reject the gospel message. The implication: any decision readers make will have significant consequences. They can either accept Jesus as the Messiah, with its mixture of purposeful suffering and new life, or, in rejection, reap their deserved punishment.

Third, such intensification of the message serves as a powerful tool of persuasion. Through Deuteronomistic-type blessings and curses, the narrator prods potential converts toward belief while encouraging current believers to stand firm in the face of persecution. Those who enter and remain a committed part of the community can expect to gain victory through their experience of suffering and renewed life. Those who reject the message or attack the community from within will be dispossessed and suffer death and decay. Thus the narrator plies effective tools of the narrative trade to attain the greatest impact possible on readers.

Conclusion

The purpose of this work has been to analyze the shape and function of the death-resurrection motif within the book of Acts. By applying William Freedman's criteria,[1] the study has both verified the presence of the motif and demonstrated its effectiveness. The function of the motif derives from its usage in the narrative and its contrast with a secondary motif of death and decay.

In order to provide an adequate summary of the findings and their implications, Freedman's criteria are described in their capacity to identify and gauge the effectiveness of the death-resurrection motif. Second, specific functions of the motif are examined. Finally, the most substantive contributions of the study are discussed.

THE SHAPE OF THE MOTIF

Though literary motifs vary from one narrative to the next, they are not amorphous. Rather, genuine motifs acquire a definite shape by displaying identifiable traits. The emphatic "telling" of Jesus's death and resurrection, as demonstrated in the diegetic analysis of ch. 1, does not create a motif. The diegetic references by themselves constitute no more than a strong theme, not a motif.[2] Yet when these statements combine with the forceful

---

1. Cf. Freedman, "Literary Motif," 123–31.

2. Cf. M. H. Abrams: "*Theme* is sometimes used interchangeably with 'motif,' but the term is more usefully applied to a general claim, or doctrine . . ." (*Glossary*, 111). Although closely related to "motif," a theme lacks the development found in the qualifications Freedman explicates and therefore should not serve as an equivalent designation for the more developed literary technique.

mimetic portrayal of the same message, as shown in chs. 2 and 3, the narrator has successfully created a literary motif.[3]

Nevertheless, presence does not guarantee effectiveness. Freedman's criteria provide a means for measuring the efficacy of the death-resurrection motif and the contrasting motif of death and decay. The fulfillment of the criteria and the intensification through contrast do reveal the clear presence of a highly potent motif.

Frequency

The death-resurrection message certainly satisfies Freedman's first requirement for an efficacious motif, which is the criterion of frequency.[4] On the diegetic level, both the narrator and protagonists regularly refer to the passion and resurrection of Jesus. Together, they explicitly characterize Jesus as the crucified-and-risen Messiah on at least ten separate occasions with many other implicit references. The message permeates the story through repetition at two different levels of narration: diegetic (the narrator's comments) and intradiegetic (the statements of the protagonists).

The frequency increases when the narrator "shows" the death-resurrection message on the mimetic level. The characters—both major (at least seven occurrences) and some of the minor (at least six occurrences)—enact the message at several points within the story, thereby increasing the number of exposures to readers. Moreover, because both major and minor characters reenact the messianic pattern, readers see the pattern recurring with different types of characters. The cumulative effect: readers receive persistent reminders of the death-resurrection message, hearing and seeing the motif at various levels within the narrative among a variety of characters.

Avoidability

The second criterion, avoidability, is satisfied through the "showing" of the messianic pattern in unexpected places. The narrator reshapes what could be typical imprisonment-release episodes, healings, and shipwreck-

---

3. Cf. Freedman, "Literary Motif," 125.
4. Ibid., 126.

rescue scenes to reflect death-resurrection sequences. Though all of these experiences have some cultural affinities with death and resurrection,[5] they do not by themselves necessitate a deeper meaning.[6] Yet, as chapters 2 and 3 demonstrate, the narrator squeezes these events into the messianic mold through the use of parallel language, symbolism, and appropriate sequencing. The diegetic references to Jesus's death and resurrection further influence the interpretation of the events, especially when connected directly to them such as the attribution of the temple beggar's healing to the crucified-and-risen Messiah.

Occurrence in Significant Contexts

The special placement of the motif further enhances its effectiveness. Either a diegetic or mimetic occurrence, or a combination of both, emerges at the beginning and ending points within the narrative and several other climactic points between.[7] The story as a whole, for example, opens with the appearances of Jesus, "presenting himself alive, after his suffering" (1:3). The narrative closes with Paul in Rome, as one of his "witnesses to the remote parts of the earth" (1:8), preaching about this same crucified-and-risen Messiah (28:31).

Within the smaller segments of the narrative, reiteration of the message continually emerges at significant junctures. When Peter begins his preaching ministry, he focuses on the crucified-and-risen Messiah (2:14–36). During climactic points of conflict, Peter himself experiences the messianic pattern through imprisonment and release (4:1–21; 5:17–41; 12:1–19). The last episode in particular, near the end of Peter's active ministry, highlights the motif.

---

5. By "cultural affinities," I am referring to ancient Mediterranean readers' propensity to associate imprisonment, shipwreck, and even lameness with death and the reversal of such circumstances with renewed life.

6. For example, when Joseph suffers imprisonment in Egypt, the narrator does not picture him as symbolically dead. Instead, Joseph remains active, supervising the business of the prison (Gen 39:21–23). Nor is his release portrayed as a resurrection experience (40:14).

7. The necessarily limited scope of this work does not allow for a detailed diagramming of all the narrative segments and specific climactic points, but the beginning and closing points within the narrative have particular significance along with those climactic points often precipitated by conflict.

106 *Conclusion*

In a similar way, the narrator punctuates the climactic points of Paul's life with either mimetic or diegetic occurrences of the motif. His conversion reflects a movement from symbolic death to resurrected life (9:1–19); his first extensive sermon accentuates the message (13:16–41); his stoning and recovery reveal a mimetic emphasis at one of the peak times of conflict (14:1–20); and Paul, like Peter, experiences a dramatic death-resurrection sequence at the end of his ministry (27:1–44).

The narrator marks other significant points of the story with the motif. One of the pivotal events at the beginning of the Jerusalem ministry is the healing of the temple beggar (3:1—4:31). And at the greatest point of direct conflict in Jerusalem,[8] Stephen suffers a death parallel to the passion of Jesus, with the expectation that Stephen, like Jesus, will one day experience resurrection (7:54–60). The "official" beginning of the gospel to the Gentiles closely binds the conversion of Cornelius to the motif (chap. 10).[9] During the farewell address of Paul at Ephesus, Eutychus vividly illustrates the long Easter message by falling three floors to his death and then returning to life in the morning hours (20:6–12). Thus, we may readily conclude that the motif certainly materializes at several key points within the Acts narrative.

Coherency

Another distinguishing characteristic of the motif is its coherency; that is, the "degree to which all instances of the motif are relevant to the principal end of the motif as a whole and to which they fit together into a recognizable and coherent unit."[10] The diegetic emphasis on Jesus's death and resurrection does indeed blend in well with the mimetic echoing of Jesus's pattern in the lives of the characters. Moreover, the narrator often ties the two events together by applying typical passion/resurrection language to the death-resurrection sequences of the characters. The temple beggar's healing serves as an example *par excellence* of this type of coherency. The healing, derived from Jesus, illustrates the messianic pattern and serves as

---

8. Tannehill labels the Stephen episode as the "Climax of the Conflict in Jerusalem" (*Narrative Unity*, 2:80).

9. Although the Ethiopian eunuch is actually the first Gentile convert, the Acts narrative draws particular attention to Cornelius as the beginning of the mission to the Gentiles.

10. Freedman, "Literary Motif," 127.

an impeccable model of Jesus's essential character. Such a high degree of coherency clearly strengthens the effect of the motif.[11]

Symbolic Appropriateness

The symbols used to describe the movement of characters from a deathlike state to renewed life also reflects an appropriate representation of the motif on the mimetic level, thereby satisfying Freedman's final criterion. For example, Freedman notes that the "constant references to doors, fences, gates, and the like are patently appropriate" to a story about "physical and spiritual isolation."[12] Changes from darkness, passivity, sleep, and lowly positions to light, activity, wakefulness, and upright stances accurately reflect the movement from death to resurrection, reinforcing the message that union with Jesus Christ logically encompasses both purposeful suffering and renewed life.

The clear fulfillment of all the criteria verifies the presence of the motif and testifies to its strength. Moreover, the secondary motif of death and decay heightens the effect of the primary motif. Just as Jesus's resurrection is contrasted with David's decay, the tragedies of Judas, Ananias and Sapphira, Simon Magus, Herod, and Elymas all provide striking negative examples in contrast to those who follow the pattern of Jesus. The distinction between the two patterns thereby creates a bold relief for readers, magnifying the impact of the primary motif.

FUNCTION OF THE MOTIF

The presence and effectiveness of a motif provide a solid framework for its function, but the specific details of its function will vary according to the message being communicated and its context. A motif of circularity may, for instance, show the futility of life, as in *Sister Carrie*, or simply offer the assurance that all creatures play an important role in the "circle of

---

11. Freedman comments, "[T]he closer the association between the components of the cluster the more unified their effect" (ibid.).

12. Ibid. He is referring to the isolation motif in *The Sound and the Fury*. Freedman also mentions on the same page that the motif of circularity is "more appropriate to a book about the circular repetitiveness of human fortune and behavior and the circular, futile strivings of the ill-equipped dreamer, as in *Sister Carrie*, than to one about, say, a love triangle." In a similar manner, reversals prove most appropriate for the depiction of the messianic pattern.

life," as in Disney's *The Lion King*. The death-resurrection motif functions to enhance the aesthetic quality of the narrative while reinforcing some basic messages for readers.

Aesthetic Value

One of the natural byproducts of all genuine motifs is the enhancement of narrative depth and reading enjoyment. As Freedman tersely describes it, the literary motif "is not an aesthetic primitive."[13] Rather, it exudes a "subtlety, richness, and complexity" desired in artistic endeavors.[14] By multiplying the level of meanings, the Lukan narrator multiplies the pleasure of the reading experience.[15] As such, Acts exhibits a richness in common with other artistic works which incorporate meaningful motifs. Simple reversals of circumstance become filled with additional meaning.

Encouragement

Undoubtedly, one of the more specific functions of the motif is to encourage Christians to endure suffering as part of their life in Christ. This encouragement comes in different ways. First, the motif assures those who experience persecution or some other form of suffering that pain is a necessary part of the Christian life. Just as Jesus suffered on the cross, so must his followers endure various types of hardships.

Paul's conversion experience and stoning at Lystra magnify this point. When speaking to Ananias about Paul, "the Lord" tells Ananias that Paul is a chosen instrument who "must suffer [δεῖ αὐτὸν ... παθεῖν] for My name's sake" (9:16). Part of this suffering is fulfilled when the people at Lystra stone Paul. The apostle's response: he encourages the Christians there by telling them, "It is through many persecutions that we must enter the kingdom of God" (14:22). According to Lukan theology, salvation is effected, at least in part, through the suffering of Jesus. The righteous suffering of his disciples clearly identifies them with their Savior.

---

13. Ibid, 129.

14. Ibid.

15. Whether or not one agrees with Richard Pervo's thesis that Luke writes in part to "delight" his readers (cf. *Profit with Delight*), the presence of the motif does reflect an artistic touch that enriches the reading experience.

Earlier in the story, the narrator makes the same point with the apostles when they suffer imprisonment. In the first instance, they compare their experience to the persecution of Jesus (4:25–29). After their second release, they go away rejoicing because "they had been considered worthy to suffer shame for his name" (5:41). The diegetic comments confirm the integral relationship between suffering and discipleship. The mimetic part of the motif then shows through numerous examples how Christians follow the pattern of Jesus's passion. As such, readers of Acts have an assurance that their suffering is not any kind of divine punishment, but an integral part of life for those who desire to enter God's reign.

Not only is righteous suffering portrayed as a blessing, the motif provides further encouragement by demonstrating that renewed life follows suffering. Just as walking follows lameness, release follows imprisonment, sight follows blindness, rescue follows shipwreck, and resurrection/resuscitation follows death, so discipleship entails the experience of revitalization. Such life does not negate the value or the pain of suffering; renewed life provides balance and hope. As the case of Stephen vividly illustrates, resuscitation does not always come in this present life, but Christians do have hope that they, like Jesus, will also move from physical death to permanent resurrection.

Warning

When the narrator shifts focus to the contrasting pattern of death and decay, the message changes to one of warning. The enemies of the church, whether inside or outside the Christian community, should beware lest they fall into permanent putrefaction. Devoted members of "The Way" may suffer, but they do not suffer decay. Opponents of God's people, however, subject themselves to the sentence of death and decay with no hope of resurrection. Judas, Ananias and Sapphira, Simon Magus, Herod, and Elymas all suffer this tragic fate as they attempt to deceive, persecute, or pervert the Christian community. Through their actions against the new people of God, they identify themselves as θεομάχοι of whom Gamaliel speaks (5:39), sounding a strong warning to would-be enemies. The narrator then graphically shows the destruction of those who refuse to heed Gamaliel's counsel. If readers of the book want to avoid the same fate, they will not disturb the growth or harmony of the church.

110 *Conclusion*

What results then is a modified Deuteronomistic history for the new people of God. The older version, found in the books Deuteronomy through Second Kings, describes the people of Israel receiving both divine blessings as a reward for their obedience to the covenant and divine punishment for their disobedience. Other Hebrew literature develops this theme by applying it to the general categories of the righteous and the wicked. Psalm 1, for example, sets forth two divergent ways of living, each with its inherent consequences: the righteous delight in the law of the Lord and will therefore prosper (vv. 1–3); in contrast, the wicked are not so and, as a result, perish (vv. 4–6).

The Acts narrative similarly records the history of the new people of God in Deuteronomistic fashion with a significant twist. The narrator divides people into two different groups, the θεόφιλοι and the θεομάχοι. Those who truly love God will accept the message of God's prophesied Messiah, Jesus. Those who follow Jesus do not simply prosper; rather, true followers experience suffering and renewed life. On the other hand, those who reject the message and persecute the Christian community become enemies of God, the θεομάχοι, and tragically suffer death and decay.

Evangelism

Consequently this Lukan version of modified Deuteronomistic history functions to persuade its readers to become true lovers/friends of God, θεόφιλοι. Paul represents the best example for them to follow. Once a vehement enemy of "The Way," he becomes its strongest advocate. His conversion reflects identification with the messianic pattern, while his later life reflects the same pattern. Though innocent of wrongdoing, he suffers on behalf of his witness for the Messiah. Yet Paul also experiences new life. Those who maintain their position as θεομάχοι, however, can expect to follow the pattern of Herod.

Other readers who seek to "worship/fear God" have different models to follow.[16] These readers do not persecute Christians, but they need to become true θεόφιλοι by believing in Jesus as the crucified-and-risen

---

16. Some scholars have begun to doubt the technical designation of σεβόμενος/ φοβούμενος τὸν θεόν (e.g., Finn, "God-Fearers," 75–84), suggesting perhaps more of a theological or literary purpose. See also MacLennan and Kraabel, "God-Fearers," 46–53.

Messiah. Cornelius serves as the paradigm for this group.[17] He first portrays in mimetic fashion the content of his conversion experience and then demonstrates his unity with the Messiah by believing in him and being baptized in the name of Jesus Christ (10:24–48). Hence, those who truly desire to "worship/fear God" should become followers of Jesus like Cornelius.

Theological Balance

The motif also creates theological balance between suffering and renewed life. Both the diegetic and mimetic parts of the motif bind the two elements closely together. Acts does not picture a painless, triumphalistic view of Christianity. Nor does the narrative isolate suffering as an end in itself. Even when Paul emphasizes his tribulations at Lystra, he is only able to do so because he "rose up" from his deathlike state (14:20). Thus, human rejection of the prophet is always followed by divine acceptance and reassurance through the bestowal of life.

CONTRIBUTIONS AND IMPLICATIONS

Despite the necessary limitations of the study, several major contributions present themselves: namely, the ability to define the shape and function of a literary motif in a biblical text. Rather than portraying an anachronistic view of Acts, the application of modern narrative theory helps clearly elucidate the theology and message of the story.

The presentation of a clear example of motif may also curb the proliferation of diluted motifs, while serving as a responsible guide for future studies. By sharpening the concept of motif, this literary term consequently becomes a much more effective tool for narrative analysis of biblical texts.

Other contributions derive from delineating the motif's various functions. Enhancement of the reading experience, encouragement, warning, evangelism, and theological balance have significant implications for the contemporary church and academic study. The present work should stimulate further dialogue on these issues and spawn interest in

17. Cf. Tyson, *Images of Judaism in Luke-Acts*, 37. Tyson believes that Cornelius is "paradigmatic of Godfearing Gentiles" who form the bulk of Luke's implied readers (36–37).

other areas such as a thorough examination of the plot in relation to the motif and its possible presence in the Third Gospel.

Moreover, the potency of the death-resurrection message as a unified motif should undoubtedly inform our understanding of Lukan soteriology and discipleship. According to the Acts narrative, salvation finds its source in both the suffering and resurrection of Jesus. Those who love God and become his followers form solidarity with him, reflecting in their lives the messianic pattern of suffering and renewed life.

Bibliography

Abrams, M. H. *A Glossary of Literary Terms*. 5th ed. New York: Holt, Rinehart, and Winston, 1988.
Adams, David Roberts. "The Suffering of Paul and the Dynamics of Luke-Acts." PhD diss., Yale University, 1979.
Aland, Kurt, Matthew Black, Carlo M. Martini, and Bruce M. Metzger, editors. *The Greek New Testament*. 4th rev. ed. Stuttgart: Bibelgesellschaft, 1998.
Alter, Robert. *The Art of Biblical Narrative*. New York: Basic Books, 1981.
Amundsen, Darrel W. "The Developing Role of Suffering in Salvation History." *Crux* 20 (1984) 12–25.
Anderson, Janice Capel. "Double and Triple Stories, the Implied Reader, and Redundancy in Matthew." *Semeia* 31 (1985) 71–89.
Anderson, Kevin L. *"But God Raised Him from the Dead": The Theology of Jesus' Resurrection in Luke-Acts*. Paternoster Biblical Monographs. Waynesboro, GA: Paternoster, 2006.
Aubert, Bernard. "The Shepherd-Flock Motif in the Miletus Discourse (Acts 20:17–38) against Its Historical Background." PhD diss., Westminster Theological Seminary, 2007.
Aune, David E. *The New Testament in Its Literary Environment*. LEC 8. Philadelphia: Westminster, 1987.
Bachmann, H., and W. A. Slaby, editors. *Computer Concordance to the Novum Testamentum Graece*. 2nd ed. Berlin: de Gruyter, 1985.
Bal, Mieke. *Narratology: Introduction to the Theory of Narrative*. Translated by Christine van Boheemen. Toronto: University of Toronto Press, 1985.
Barrett, C. K. *The Acts of the Apostles*. ICC. New York: T. & T. Clark, 2002.
———. "Theologia Crucis—in Acts?" In *Theologia Crucis, Signum Crucis: Festschrift für Erich Dinkler zum 70*, edited by Carl Andresen and Günter Klein, 73–84. Tübingen: Mohr, 1979.
Battenhouse, Roy. "The Tragedy of Absalom." *ChrLit* 31 (1982) 53–57.
Bauer, Walter, Frederick William Danker, W. F. Arndt, and F. W. Gingrich, editors. *A Greek-English Lexicon of the New Testament and Other Early Christian Literature*. 3rd ed. Chicago: University of Chicago Press, 2000.
Beasley-Murray, George. *Baptism in the New Testament*. Grand Rapids: Eerdmans, 1962.
Berkowitz, Luci, and Karl A. Squitier, editors. *Thesaurus linguae graecae: Canon of Greek Authors and Works*. 2nd ed. Oxford: Oxford University Press, 1986.

Bock, Darrell L. *Acts*. Baker Exegetical Commentary of the New Testament. Grand Rapids: Baker Academic, 2007.

Booth, Wayne C. *The Rhetoric of Fiction*. 2nd ed. Chicago: University of Chicago Press, 1983.

Bovon, François. *Luke the Theologian (1950–2005)*. 2nd rev. ed. Waco, TX: Baylor University Press, 2006.

Braumann, Georg. "Das Mittel der Zeit: Erwägungen zur Theologie des Lukasevangeliums." *ZNW* 54 (1963) 117–45.

Brawley, Robert L. *Centering on God: Method and Message in Luke-Acts*. Literary Currents in Biblical Interpretation. Louisville: Westminster John Knox, 1990.

Brock, Rita Nakashima, and Rebecca Ann Parker. *Proverbs of Ashes: Violence, Redemptive Suffering, and the Search for What Saves Us*. Boston: Beacon, 2001.

Brown, E. K. *Rhythm in the Novel*. Alexander Lectures, 1949–50. Toronto: University of Toronto Press, 1950.

Brown, Francis, S. R. Driver, and Charles A. Briggs, editors *A Hebrew and English Lexicon of the Old Testament: With an Appendix Containing the Biblical Aramaic*. Oxford, 1907.

Bruce, F. F. *The Acts of the Apostles: The Greek Text with Introduction and Commentary*. 3rd ed. Grand Rapids: Eerdmans, 1990.

———. *The Book of Acts*. NICNT. Rev. ed. Grand Rapids: Eerdmans, 1988.

Burnett, Fred W. "Prolegomenon to Reading Matthew's Eschatological Discourse: Redundancy and the Education of the Reader in Matthew." *Semeia* 31 (1985) 91–109.

Cadbury, Henry J. *The Making of Luke-Acts*. 2nd ed. London: SPCK, 1958.

———. "The Speeches in Acts." In *The Beginnings of Christianity*, edited by Kirsopp Lake and H. J. Cadbury, 5:402–27. London: MacMillan, 1933.

———. *The Style and Literary Method of Luke*. Cambridge: Harvard University Press, 1913.

Carpenter, Ronald H. "Stylistic Redundancy and Function in Discourse." *Language and Style* 3 (1970) 62–68.

Chamberlain, Daniel Frank. *Narrative Perspective in Fiction: A Phenomenological Mediation of Reader, Text, and World*. University of Toronto Romance Series 59. Toronto: University of Toronto Press, 1990.

Chatman, Seymour Benjamin. *Coming to Terms: The Rhetoric of Narrative in Fiction and Film*. Ithaca, NY: Cornell University Press, 1990.

———. *Story and Discourse: Narrative Structure in Fiction and Film*. Ithaca, NY: Cornell University Press, 1978.

Clements, Ronald E. "Patterns in the Prophetic Canon: Healing the Blind and the Lame." In *Canon, Theology, and Old Testament Interpretation: Essays in Honor of Brevard S. Childs*, edited by Gene M. Tucker, David L. Peterson, and Robert R. Wilson, 189–200. Philadelphia: Fortress, 1988.

Cohan, Steven, and Linda M. Shires. *Telling Stories: A Theoretical Analysis of Narrative Fiction*. New Accents. New York: Routledge, 1988.

Cohn, Robert L. "Form and Perspective in 2 Kings 5." *VT* 33 (1983) 171–84.

Conzelmann, Hans. *Acts of the Apostles: A Commentary*. Translated by James Limburg, A. Thomas Kraabel, and Donald H. Juel. Hermeneia. Philadelphia: Fortress, 1987.

———. *The Theology of St. Luke*. Translated by Geoffrey Buswell. New York: Harper & Row, 1961.

Cosgrove, Charles. "The Divine Δεῖ in Luke-Acts." *NovT* 26 (1984) 168–90.

Cranford, Lorin L. *Exegeting the New Testament: Research Update with Research Bibliography*. Vol. 2. Fort Worth, TX: Scripta, 1991.
Creed, John Martin. *The Gospel according to St. Luke: The Greek Text with Introduction, Notes, and Indices*. London: MacMillan, 1930.
Culpepper, R. Alan. *Anatomy of the Fourth Gospel: A Study in Literary Design*. FF New Testament. Philadelphia: Fortress, 1983.
Cunningham, Scott. *"Through Many Tribulations": The Theology of Persecution in Luke-Acts*. JSNTSup 142. Sheffield: Sheffield Academic, 1997.
Dawsey, James M. *The Lukan Voice: Confusion and Irony in the Gospel of Luke*. Macon, GA: Mercer University Press, 1986.
Dibble, Charles L. "Primitive Symbolism in the Breaking of Bread." *ATR* 5 (1922–23) 187–210.
Dibelius, Martin. *Studies in the Acts of the Apostles*. Edited by Heinrich Greeven. Translated by Mary Ling. New York: Scribner, 1956.
Dillon, Richard J. *From Eye-Witnesses to Ministers of the Word: Tradition and Composition in Luke 24*. AnBib 82. Rome: Biblical Institute Press, 1978.
Dodd, C. H. *The Apostolic Preaching and Its Developments, Three Lectures*. London: Hodder & Stoughton, 1936.
Dornseiff, Franz. "Lukas der Schriftsteller." *ZNW* 35 (1936) 129–55.
Dunn, James D. G. *The Acts of the Apostles*. Narrative Commentaries. Valley Forge, PA: Trinity, 1996.
———. *Romans 1–8*. WBC 38A. Dallas: Word, 1988.
Dupont, J. "L'utilisation apologétique de l'Ancien Testament dans les discours des Actes." In *Analecta Lovaniensia Biblica et Orientalia*. Paris: Louvain, 1953.
Ehrhardt, Arnold. *The Acts of the Apostles: Ten Lectures*. Manchester: Manchester University Press, 1969.
Eliade, Mircea. *Images and Symbols: Studies in Religious Symbolism*. Translated by Philip Mairet. New York: Sheed & Ward, 1961.
Elledge, Casey Deryl. "Resurrection and the End of History: The Resurrection Motif in Paul's Preaching and Defense in the Acts of the Apostles." PhD diss., Princeton Theological Seminary, 2001.
Elliott, John. "Temple versus Household in Luke-Acts." *HvTSt* 47 (1991) 88–120.
Engelbrecht, J. "Trends in Miracle Research." *Neot* 22 (1988) 139–61.
Esler, Philip Francis. *Community and Gospel in Luke-Acts: The Social and Political Motivations of Lucan Theology*. SNTSMS 57. Cambridge: Cambridge University Press, 1987.
Estridge, Charles A. "Suffering in Contexts of the Speeches of Acts." PhD diss., Baylor University, 1991.
Farbridge, Marice H. *Studies in Biblical and Semitic Symbolism*. Library of Biblical Studies. New York: Ktav, 1970.
Finn, Thomas M. "The God-Fearers Reconsidered." *CBQ* 47 (1985) 75–84.
Fishelis, Avrohom, and Shmuel Fishelis. *Judges: A New Translation*. Judaica Books of the Prophets. New York: Judaica, 1979.
Fitzmyer, Joseph. "David, 'Being Therefore a Prophet . . .' (Acts 2:30)." *CBQ* 34 (1972) 332–39.
———. *The Gospel according to Luke: Introduction, Translation, and Notes*. 2 vols. AB 28-28A. Garden City, NY: Doubleday, 1981–85.

Flender, Helmut. *St. Luke: Theologian of Redemptive History.* Translated by Reginald H. Fuller and Ilse Fuller. Philadelphia: Fortress, 1967.

Forster, E. M. *Aspects of the Novel.* London: E. Arnold, 1927.

Freedman, William. "The Literary Motif: A Definition and Evaluation." *Novel* 4 (1971) 123–31.

———. "A Look at Dreiser as Artist: The Motif of Circularity in *Sister Carrie*." *Modern Fiction Studies* 8 (1962) 384–92.

Frein, Brigid. "The Literary Significance of the Jesus-as-Prophet Motif in the Gospel of Luke and the Acts of the Apostles." PhD diss., Saint Louis University, 1989.

Funk, Robert W. *The Poetics of Biblical Narrative.* FF Literary Facets. Sonoma, CA: Polebridge, 1988.

Gardner, Percy. "The Speeches of St. Paul in Acts." In *Essays on Some Biblical Questions of the Day: By Members of the University of Cambridge,* edited by Henry Barclay Swete, 379–419. London: MacMillan, 1909.

Garrett, Susan R. *The Demise of the Devil: Magic and the Demonic in Luke's Writings.* Minneapolis: Fortress, 1989.

———. "Exodus from Bondage: Luke 9:31 and Acts 12:1–24." *CBQ* 52 (1990) 670–77.

Gasque, W. Ward. *A History of the Interpretation of the Acts of the Apostles.* Rev. ed. Peabody, MA: Hendrickson, 1989.

Gaventa, Beverly Roberts. *The Acts of the Apostles.* ANTC. Nashville: Abingdon, 2003.

———. *From Darkness to Light: Aspects of Conversion in the New Testament.* OBT 20. Philadelphia: Fortress, 1986.

———. "The Overthrown Enemy: Luke's Portrait of Paul." In *SBLSP* (1985), edited by Kent H. Richards, 439–49. Atlanta: Scholars, 1985.

———. "'To Speak Thy Word with Boldness,' Acts 4:23–31." *Faith and Mission* 3 (1986) 79.

———. "Toward a Theology of Acts: Reading and Rereading." *Int* 42 (1988) 146–57.

Genette, Gérard. *Narrative Discourse: An Essay in Method.* Translated by Jane E. Lewin. Ithaca, NY: Cornell University Press, 1980.

———. *Narrative Discourse Revisited.* Translated by Jane E. Lewin. Ithaca, NY: Cornell University Press, 1988.

Giblin, C. H. "Complementarity of Symbolic Event and Discourse in Acts 2:1–40." *ScEs* 6 (1969) 189–96.

Glöckner, Richard. *Die Verkündigung des Heils beim Evangelisten Lukas.* Walberger Studien der Albertus-Magnus-Akademie: Theologische Reihe 9. Mainz: Grünewald, 1976.

Goulder, M. D. *Type and History in Acts.* London: SPCK, 1964.

Gowler, David B. *Host, Guest, Enemy, and Friend: Portraits of the Pharisees in Luke and Acts.* Emory Studies in Early Christianity 2. New York: Lang, 1991.

Green, Joel B. "The Death of Jesus and the Ways of God." *Int* 52 (1998) 24–37.

———. "'Witnesses of His Resurrection': Resurrection, Salvation, Discipleship, and Mission in the Acts of the Apostles." In *Life in the Face of Death: The Resurrection Message of the New Testament,* edited by Richard N. Longenecker, 227–46. McMaster New Testament Studies. Grand Rapids: Eerdmans, 1998.

Grumm, Minert H. "Another Look at Acts." *ExpTim* 96 (1985) 333–37.

Habel, Norman C. *The Book of Job.* Philadelphia: Westminster, 1985.

Haenchen, Ernst. *The Acts of the Apostles: A Commentary.* Translated by Bernard Noble et al. Philadelphia: Westminster, 1971.

Hamm, M. Dennis. "Acts 3,1–10: The Healing of the Temple Beggar as Lucan Theology." *Biblica* 67 (1986) 305–9.

———. "Acts 3:12–26: Peter's Speech and the Healing of the Man Born Lame." *PRSt* 11 (1984) 199–217.

———. "Paul's Blindness and Its Healing: Clues to Symbolic Intent (Acts 9:22 and 26)." *Biblica* 71 (1990) 63–72.

Harvey, John D. "The 'With Christ' Motif in Paul's Thought." *JETS* 35 (1992) 329–40.

Hemer, Colin J. *The Book of Acts in the Setting of Hellenistic History*. Edited by Conrad H. Gempf. WUNT 49. Winona Lake, IN: Eisenbrauns, 1990.

———. "The Speeches of Acts." *TynBul* 40 (1989) 76–85.

Hilgert, Earle. *The Ship and Related Symbols in the New Testament*. Assen: Royal Vangorcum, 1962.

Hooker, Morna D. *Not Ashamed of the Gospel: New Testament Interpretations of the Death of Christ*. Didsbury Lectures 1988. Grand Rapids: Eerdmans, 1994.

Horsley, G. H. R. "Speeches and Dialogue in Acts." *NTS* 32 (1986) 609–14.

House, Paul R. "Suffering and the Purpose of Acts." *JETS* 33 (1990) 317–30.

Iser, Wolfgang. *The Implied Reader: Patterns of Communication in Prose Fiction from Bunyan to Beckett*. Baltimore: Johns Hopkins University Press, 1974.

Johnson, Luke Timothy. *The Acts of the Apostles*. SP 5. Collegeville, MN: Liturgical, 1992.

———. *The Literary Function of Possessions in Luke-Acts*. SBLDS 39. Missoula, MT: Scholars, 1977.

Johnson, Steven Robert. "Markan Miracle Models of Suffering, Death, and Resurrection." M.A. thesis, Miami University, Ohio, 1991.

Judisch, Douglas. "Propitiation in the Language and Typology of the Old Testament." *CTQ* 48 (1984) 221–43.

Käsemann, Ernst. *Essays on New Testament Themes*. Translated by W. J. Montague. SBT 41. London: SCM, 1964.

Kawin, Bruce F. *Telling It Again and Again: Repetition in Literature and Film*. Ithaca, NY: Cornell University Press, 1972.

Keathley, Naymond H., editor. *With Steadfast Purpose: Essays on Acts in Honor of Henry Jackson Flanders, Jr*. Waco, TX: Baylor University Press, 1990.

Keel, Othmar. *The Symbolism of the Biblical World: Aancient Near Eastern Iconography and the Book of Psalm*. Translated by Timothy J. Hallett. New York: Seabury, 1978.

Kermode, Frank. *The Genesis of Secrecy: On the Interpretation of Narrative*. Charles Eliot Norton Lectures, 1977–78. Cambridge: Harvard University Press, 1979.

Kilgallen, John J. "Acts 13:38–39: Culmination of Paul's Speech in Pisidia." *Biblica* 69 (1988) 480–506.

———. "What the Apostles Proclaimed at Acts 4,2." In *Resurrection in the New Testament: Festschrift J. Lambrecht*, edited by R. Bieringer et al., 233–48. BETL 165. Leuven: Leuven University Press, 2002.

Kim, Hyochan Michael. "'From Israel to the Nations': A Critical Study of the Abraham Motif in Luke-Acts." PhD diss., Trinity Evangelical Divinity School, 2007.

Kingsbury, Jack Dean. *Conflict in Luke: Jesus, Authorities, Disciples*. Minneapolis: Fortress, 1991.

Kolasny, Judette Marie. "Pericopes of Confrontation and Rejection as a Plot Devise in Luke-Acts." PhD diss., Marquette University, 1985.

Kränkl, Emmeram. *Jesus der Knecht Gottes: Die heilsgeschichtliche Stellung Jesu in den Reden der Apostelgeschichte*. Biblische Untersuchungen 8. Regensburg: Pustet, 1972.

Krašovec, Jože. *Antithetic Structure in Biblical Hebrew Poetry*. VTSup 35. Leiden: Brill, 1984.

Kremer, J. "Wir alle werden leben." *StZ* 208 (1990) 733–44.

Kurz, William S. "Narrative Approaches to Luke-Acts." *Biblica* 68 (1987) 195–220.

———. "The Function of Christological Proof from Prophecy for Luke and Justin." PhD diss., Yale University, 1976.

Ladouceur, David. "Hellenistic Preconceptions of Shipwreck and Pollution as a Concept for Acts 27–28." *HTR* 73 (1980) 435–49.

Lanser, Susan Sniader. *The Narrative Act: Point of View in Prose Fiction*. Princeton: Princeton University Press, 1981.

Lasine, Stuart. "Guest and Host in Judges 19." *JSOT* 29 (1984) 37–59.

Léon-Dufour, Xavier. *Life and Death in the New Testament*. Translated by Terrence Prendergast. San Francisco: Harper & Row, 1986.

Longenecker, Richard N. "Taking Up the Cross Daily: Discipleship in Luke-Acts." In *Patterns of Discipleship in the New Testament*, edited by Richard N. Longenecker, 50–76. McMaster New Testament Studies. Grand Rapids: Eerdmans, 1996.

Longman, Tremper, III. *Literary Approaches to Biblical Interpretation*. Vol. 3, *Foundations of Contemporary Interpretation*. Edited by Moisés Silva. Grand Rapids: Academie, 1987.

Louw, Johannes P., and Eugene A. Nida. *Greek-English Lexicon of the New Testament: Based on Semantic Domains*. 2 vols. 2nd ed. New York: United Bible Societies, 1989.

Lüdemann, Gerd. *The Acts of the Apostles: What Really Happened in the Earliest Days of the Church*. Amherst, NY: Prometheus, 2005.

Lowth, Robert. *Lectures on the Sacred Poetry of the Hebrews*. Translated by G. Gregory. London: Chadwick, 1847.

MacLennan, Robert S., and A. Thomas Kraabel. "The God-Fearers—A Literary and Theological Invention." *BAR* 12.5 (1986) 46–53.

Maddox, Robert. *The Purpose of Luke-Acts*. Studies of the New Testament and Its World. Edinburgh: T. & T. Clark, 1982.

Malbon, Elizabeth Struthers. *Narrative Space and Mythic Meaning in Mark*. New Voices in Biblical Studies. San Francisco: Harper & Row, 1986.

Malina, Bruce J., and John J. Pilch. *Social-Science Commentary on the Book of Acts*. Minneapolis: Fortress, 2008.

Marguerat, Daniel. "La Mort D'Ananias et Saphira (Ac 5.1–11)." *NTS* 39 (1993) 222–25.

Marshall, I. Howard. *The Acts of the Apostles: An Introduction and Commentary*. TNTC 5. Grand Rapids: Eerdmans, 1980.

———. *Luke: Historian and Theologian*. London: Paternoster, 1970.

———. "The Resurrection in the Acts of the Apostles." In *Apostolic History and the Gospel: Biblical and Historical Essays Presented to F. F. Bruce on His 60th Birthday*, edited by W. Ward Gasque and Ralph P. Martin, 92–107. Grand Rapids: Eerdmans, 1970.

Martin, Ralph P. *Second Corinthians*. WBC 40. Dallas: Word, 1982.

Mattill, A. J., Jr. "The Jesus-Paul Parallels and the Purpose of Luke-Acts." *NovT* 17 (1975) 15–46.

———, and Mary Bedford Mattill, compilers. *A Classified Bibliography of Literature on the Acts of the Apostles*. NTTS 7. Leiden: Brill, 1966.

McMahan, Craig Thomas. "Meals as Type-Scenes in the Gospel of Luke." PhD diss., Southern Baptist Theological Seminary, 1987.

Mealand, D. L. "Hellenistic Historians and the Style of Acts." *ZNW* 82 (1991) 42–66.

Meyer, Marvin W., editor. *The Ancient Mysteries: A Sourcebook, Sacred Texts of the Mystery Religions of the Ancient Mediterranean World.* San Francisco: Harper & Row, 1987.
Miller, J. Hillis, editor. *Aspects of Narrative: Selected Papers from the English Institute.* New York: Columbia University Press, 1971.
———. *Fiction and Repetition: Seven English Novels.* Cambridge: Harvard University Press, 1982.
Mills, Watson E. *A Bibliography of the Periodical Literature on the Acts of the Apostles 1962–1984.* NovTSup 58. Leiden: Brill, 1986.
Minear, Paul Sevier. *To Heal and to Reveal: The Prophetic Vocation according to Luke.* New York: Seabury, 1976.
Mittelstadt, Martin W. *Spirit and Suffering in Luke-Acts: Implications for a Pentecostal Pneumatology.* Journal of Pentecostal Theology Supplement Series 26. London: T. & T. Clark, 2004.
Moessner, David P. "'The Christ Must Suffer': New Light on the Jesus-Peter, Stephen, Paul Parallels in Luke-Acts." *NovT* 28 (1986) 220–56.
———. "'The Christ Must Suffer,' The Church Must Suffer: Rethinking the Theology of the Cross in Luke-Acts." In *SBLSP* (1990), 165–95. Atlanta: Scholars, 1990.
———. *Lord of the Banquet: The Literary and Theological Significance of the Lukan Travel Narrative.* Minneapolis: Fortress, 1989.
———. "Paul and the Pattern of the Prophet like Moses in Acts." In *SBLSP* (1983), 203–12. Chico, CA: Scholars, 1983.
Moore, Stephen D. *Literary Criticism and the Gospels: The Theoretical Challenge.* New Haven: Yale University Press, 1989.
Moule, C. F. D. "From Defendant to Judge—and Deliverer." In *The Phenomenon of the New Testament: An Inquiry into the Implications of Certain Features of the New Testament.* SBT 2/1. Naperville, IL: Allenson, 1967.
Munck, Johannes. *The Acts of the Apostles.* AB 31. Garden City, NY: Doubleday, 1967.
Murray, Patrick. *Literary Criticism: A Glossary of Major Terms.* London: Longman, 1978.
Neirynck, Frans. "The Miracle Stories in the Acts of the Apostles." In *Les Actes des Apôtres: Traditions, rédaction, théologie,* edited by J. Kremer, 169–213. BETL 48. Gembloux: Leuven University Press, 1979.
Nestle, Wilhelm. "Legenden vom Tod der Gottesverächter." *AR* 33 (1936) 246–69.
Neyrey, Jerome. *The Passion According to Luke: A Redaction Study of Luke's Soteriology.* Theological Inquiries. New York: Paulist, 1985.
O'Toole, Robert F. "Christ's Resurrection in Acts 13:13–52." *Biblica* 60 (1979) 361–72.
———. "Luke's Notion of 'Be Imitators of Me as I Am of Christ' in Acts 25–26." *BTB* 8 (1978) 153–61.
———. "Luke's Understanding of Jesus' Resurrection-Ascension-Exaltation." *BTB* 9 (1979) 106–14.
———. "Parallels between Jesus and His Disciples in Luke-Acts: A Further Study." *Biblische Zeitschrift* 27 (1983) 195–212.
———. "Some Observations on *Anistēmi,* 'I Raise,' in Acts 3:22, 26." *ScEs* 31 (1979) 85–92.
———. *The Unity of Luke's Theology: An Analysis of Luke-Acts.* GNS 9. Wilmington, DE: Glazier, 1984.
Owen, H. P. "Stephen's Vision in Acts VII 55–6." *NTS* (1954–55) 224–26.
Parsons, Mikeal C. *Acts.* Paideia. Grand Rapids: Baker Academic, 2008.

———. "Christian Origins and Narrative Openings: The Sense of a Beginning in Acts 1–5." *RevExp* 87 (1990) 403–22.

———. *The Departure of Jesus in Luke-Acts: The Ascension Narratives in Context*. JSNTSup 21. Sheffield: JSOT Press, 1987.

———. "The Unity of the Lukan Writings: Rethinking the *Opinio Communis*." In *With Steadfast Purpose: Essays in Honor of Henry Jackson Flanders, Jr.*, edited by Naymond H. Keathley, 29–53. Waco, TX: Baylor University Press, 1990.

———, and Joseph B. Tyson, editors. *Cadbury, Knox, and Talbert: American Contributions to the Study of Acts*. SBLCP. Atlanta: Scholars, 1992.

———, and Richard I. Pervo. *Rethinking the Unity of Luke and Acts*. Minneapolis: Fortress, 1993.

Patterson, Stephen J. *Beyond the Passion: Rethinking the Death and Life of Jesus*. Minneapolis: Fortress, 2004.

Pelikan, Jaroslav. *Acts*. Brazos Theological Commentary on the Bible. Grand Rapids: Brazos, 2005.

Pervo, Richard I. *Acts: A Commentary*. Hermeneia. Minneapolis: Fortress, 2008.

———. *Luke's Story of Paul*. Minneapolis: Fortress, 1990.

———. *Profit with Delight: The Literary Genre of the Acts of the Apostles*. Philadelphia: Fortress, 1987.

Petersen, Norman R. *Literary Criticism for New Testament Critics*. GBS New Testament. Philadelphia: Fortress, 1978.

Philostratus. *Life of Apollonius of Tyana*. Translated by F. C. Conybeare. 2 vols. LCL. Cambridge: Harvard University Press, 1948.

Pilch, John J. "Sickness and Healing in Luke-Acts." In *The Social World of Luke-Acts: Models for Interpretation*, edited by Jerome H. Neyrey, 181–209. Peabody, MA: Hendrickson, 1991.

Polhill, John B. *Acts*. NAC 26. Nashville: Broadman, 1992.

Porter, R. J. "What Did Philip Say to the Eunuch?" *ExpTim* 100 (1988) 55.

Powell, Mark Allan. *The Bible and Modern Literary Criticism: A Critical Assessment and Annotated Bibliography*. Bibliographies and Indexes in Religious Studies 22. New York: Greenwood, 1992.

———. *What Are They Saying about Acts?* New York: Paulist, 1991.

———. *What Are They Saying about Luke?* New York: Paulist, 1989.

———. *What Is Narrative Criticism?* GBS New Testament. Minneapolis: Fortress, 1990.

Praeder, Susan Marie. "Jesus-Paul, Peter-Paul, and Jesus-Peter Parallelisms in Luke-Acts." In *SBLSP* (1984), 23–39. Chico, CA: Scholars, 1984.

———. "Miracle Stories in Christian Antiquity: Some Narrative Elements." *Forum* 2 (1986) 43–54.

———. "The Narrative Voyage: An Analysis and Interpretation of Acts 27–28." PhD diss., Graduate Theological Union, 1980.

Prinsloo, Willem S. "Isaiah 14:12–15: Humiliation, Hubris, Humiliation." *ZAW* 93 (1981) 432–38.

Puskas, Charles B. *The Conclusion of Luke-Acts: The Significance of Acts 28:16–31*. Eugene, OR: Pickwick, 2009.

Rackham, Richard Belward. *The Acts of the Apostles: An Exposition*. 2nd ed. WC. London: Methuen, 1904.

Radl, Walter. *Paulus und Jesus im Lukanischen Doppelwerk: Untersuchungen zu Parallelmotiven im Lukasevangelium und in der Apostelgeschichte*. Europäische Hochschulschriften 23:49. Bern: Lang, 1975.

Ramsey, George. "Plots, Gaps, Repetitions, and Ambiguity in Luke 15." *PRSt* 17 (1990) 33–42.

Reeves, Rodney. "To Be or Not to Be? That is Not the Question: Paul's Choice in Philippians 1:22." *PRSt* 19 (1992) 286–87.

Reicke, Bo. "The Risen Lord and His Church: The Theology of Acts." *Int* 13 (1959) 156–69.

Rhoads, David M., and Donald Michie. *Mark as Story: An Introduction to the Narrative of a Gospel*. Philadelphia: Fortress, 1982.

Richard, Earl. *Acts 6:1—8:4: The Author's Method of Composition*. SBLDS 41. Missoula, MT: Scholars, 1978.

———. "The Old Testament in Acts: Wilcox's Semitisms in Retrospect." *CBQ* 42 (1980) 330–41.

Ridderbos, Herman N. *The Speeches of Peter in the Acts of the Apostles*. Tyndale New Testament Lecture 1961. London: Tyndale, 1961.

Rimmon-Kenan, Shlomith. *Narrative Fiction: Contemporary Poetics*. New Accents. New York: Methuen, 1983.

Robinson, Anthony B., and Robert W. Wall. *Called to Be Church: The Book of Acts for a New Day*. Grand Rapids: Eerdmans, 2006.

Rowe, C. Kavin. "Acts 2.36 and the Continuity of Lukan Christology." *NTS* 53 (2007) 37–56.

Ryken, Leland, editor. *The New Testament in Literary Criticism*. Library of Literary Criticism. New York: Ungar, 1984.

Sabugal, S. "El vocabulario Anastasiologico del Nuevo Testamento." *Revista Agustiniana* 30 (1989) 385–401.

Samain, P. "L'Accusation de magie contre le Christ dans les évangiles." *ETL* 15 (1938) 454–55.

Sanders, Jack N. "Peter and Paul in the Acts." *NTS* 2 (1955–56) 133–43.

Sandmel, Samuel. "Parallelomania." *JBL* 81 (1962) 1–13.

Savran, George W. *Telling and Retelling: Quotation in Biblical Narrative*. Indiana Studies in Biblical Literature. Bloomington: Indiana University Press, 1988.

Scheffler, Even Hans. "Suffering in Luke's Gospel." PhD diss., University of Pretoria, 1989.

Scroggs, Robin. "Baptism in Mark: Dying and Rising with Christ." *JBL* 92 (1973) 536–37.

Schütz, F. *Der leidende Christus: Die angefochtene Gemeinde und das Christuskerygma der lukanischen Schriften*. BWANT 92. Stuttgart: Kohhammer, 1969.

Sheeley, S. M. "Narrative Asides and Narrative Authority in Luke-Acts." *BTB* 18 (1988) 102–7.

Stagg, Frank. *The Book of Acts: The Early Struggle for an Unhindered Gospel*. Nashville: Broadman, 1955.

Sternberg, Meir. *Expositional Modes and Temporal Ordering in Fiction*. Baltimore: Johns Hopkins University Press, 1978.

———. *The Poetics of Biblical Narrative: Ideological Literature and the Drama of Reading*. Indiana Literary Biblical Series. Bloomington: Indiana University Press, 1985.

Stoops, Robert F., Jr. "Riot and Assembly: The Social Context of Acts 19:23–41." *JBL* 108 (1989) 73–91.

Strobel, August. "Passa-Symbolik und Passa-Wunder in Acts XII. 3ff." *NTS* 4 (1957–1958) 210–15.
Suleiman, Susan Rubin. "Redundancy and the 'Readable Text.'" *Poetics Today* 1 (1980) 119–42.
Talbert, Charles H. *Literary Patterns, Theological Themes, and the Genre of Luke-Acts.* SBLMS 20. Missoula, MT: Scholars, 1974.
———, editor. *Luke-Acts: New Perspectives from the Society of Biblical Literature Seminar.* New York: Crossroad, 1984.
———, editor. *Perspectives on Luke-Acts.* Edinburgh: T. & T. Clark, 1978.
———. *Reading Acts: A Literary and Theological Commentary on the Acts of the Apostles.* Rev. ed. Macon, GA: Smyth & Helwys, 2005.
———. *Romans.* Smyth & Helwys Biblical Commentary. Macon, GA: Smyth & Helwys, 2005.
Tannehill, Robert C. "The Composition of Acts 3–5: Narrative Development and Echo Effect." In *SBLSP* (1984), 217–40. Chico, CA: Scholars, 1984.
———. *Dying and Rising with Christ: A Study in Pauline Theology.* BZNW 32. 1967. Reprinted, Eugene, OR: Wipf & Stock, 2006.
———. *The Narrative Unity of Luke-Acts: A Literary Interpretation.* 2 vols. FF. Philadelphia: Fortress, 1986–90.
Terrell, Joanne Marie. *Power in the Blood? The Cross in the African American Experience.* 1998. Reprinted, Eugene, OR: Wipf & Stock, 2005.
Tiede, David L. *Prophecy and History in Luke-Acts.* Philadelphia: Fortress, 1980.
Thompson, Deanna A. *Crossing the Divide: Luther, Feminism, and the Cross.* Minneapolis: Fortress, 2004.
Trémel, Bernard. "À propos d'Actes 20,7–12: Puissance du thaumaturge ou du témoin?" *RTP* 112 (1980) 359–69.
Trocmé, étienne. *Le Livre des Acts et l'Histoire.* Paris: Presses Universitaires de France, 1957.
Tuckett, Christopher M. "The Christology of Luke-Acts." In *The Unity of Luke-Acts*, edited by Joseph Verheyden, 133–64. BETL 142. Leuven: Leuven University Press, 1999.
Tyson, Joseph B. *The Death of Jesus in Luke-Acts.* Columbia: University of South Carolina Press, 1986.
———. *Images of Judaism in Luke-Acts.* Columbia: University of South Carolina Press, 1992.
———, editor. *Luke-Acts and the Jewish People: Eight Critical Perspectives.* Minneapolis: Augsburg, 1988.
———. Review of *The Lukan Voice: Confusion and Irony in the Gospel of Luke*, by James M. Dawsey. *JBL* 107 (1988) 545.
Uspensky, Boris. *A Poetics of Composition: The Structure of the Artistic Text and Typology of a Compositional Form.* Translated by Valentina Zavarin and Susan Wittig. Berkeley: University of California Press, 1973.
Viviano, Benedict T., and Justin Taylor. "Sadducees, Angels, and Resurrection." *JBL* 111 (1992) 496–98.
Wagner, Günter, editor. *An Exegetical Bibliography of the New Testament: Luke and Acts.* Vol. 2. Macon, GA: Mercer University Press, 1985.
Walaskay, Paul W. *Acts.* Westminster Bible Companion. Louisville: Westminster John Knox, 1998.

Walworth, Allen. "The Narrator of Acts." PhD diss., Southern Baptist Theological Seminary, 1984.
Wanke, Joachim. *Beobachtungen zum Eucharistieverständnis des Lukas auf Grund der lukanischen Mahlberichte.* Leipzig: St. Benno, 1973.
Weaver, J. Denny. *The Nonviolent Atonement.* Grand Rapids: Eerdmans, 2001.
Weiser, Artur. *The Psalms.* Translated by Herbert Hartwell. Old Testament Library. Philadelphia: Westminster, 1962.
Westermann, Claus. *The Living Psalms.* Translated by J. R. Porter. Grand Rapids: Eerdmans, 1989.
Wheelwright, Philip Ellis. *Metaphor & Reality.* Bloomington: Indiana University Press, 1962.
Williams, David John. *Acts.* NIBCNT 5. Peabody, MA: Hendrickson, 1985
Williams, Sam K. *Jesus' Death as Saving Event: The Background and Origin of a Concept.* HDR 2. Missoula, MT: Scholars, 1975.
Witherington, Ben III. *The Acts of the Apostles: A Socio-Rhetorical Commentary.* Grand Rapids: Eerdmans, 1998.
Wittig, Susan. "Formulaic Style and the Problem of Redundancy." *Centrum* 1 (1973) 123–36.
Xenophon. *Ephesian Tale.* In *Collected Ancient Greek Novels*, edited by B. P. Reardon, 125–69. Berkeley: University of California Press, 1989.
Zehnle, Richard. *Peter's Pentecost Discourse: Tradition and Lukan Reinterpretation in Peter's Speeches of Acts 2 and 3.* SBLMS 15. Nashville: Abingdon, 1971.
Zeller, Eduard. *The Contents and Origin of the Acts of the Apostles, Critically Investigated.* Vol. 2. Theological Translation Fund Library 8, 10. London: Williams & Norgate, 1875–76.

Index of Modern Authors

Abrams, M. H., 22, 103n2
Alter, R., 10n45, 24n50, 40n5, 65n19, 72n49
Anderson, J. C., 10n45, 40n5, 49, 72
Anderson, K. L., 3-4, 5n24
Aubert, B., 1n2

Bachmann, H., 33n78
Barrett, C. K., 6
Battenhouse, R., 81n7
Beasley-Murray, G., 76, 77n65
Braumann, G., 4
Brock, R. N., 5n27
Bruce, F. F., 17, 65n17, 73n53, 88, 94nn68-69
Burnett, F., 10n45, 40n5

Cohn, R. L., 81n8
Conzelmann, H., 9n43, 16, 25, 26n54, 50n48, 64, 73nn52-53, 76n62, 86n36, 87-88, 90n54, 95n71, 96n77,
Cosgrove, C. H., 19, 28, 29n67
Creed, J. M., 3
Culpepper, R. A., xvi, 2n7, 15n8, 27n63, 39n2, 61n2, 81n11
Cunningham, S., 5-6

Dawsey, J., 14
Dibelius, M., 75n59
Dillon, R. J., 19n25
Dodd, C. H., 3, 22
Dornseiff, F., 49n40
Dreiser, T., 7, 8n39, 45n29, 48n37
Dunn, J. D. G., 81n9

Ehrhardt, A., 94n69
Eliade, M., 57
Elledge, C. D., 1n2
Elliott, J., 81n17
Esler, P., 75
Estridge, C. A., 4, 5n23

Farbridge, M. H., 69, 70n41
Finn, T. M., 110n16
Fishelis, A., 91n56
Fishelis, S., 91n56
Fitzmyer, J., 84n27
Freedman, W., xv-xvi, 1-2, 7-9, 11, 22-23, 38, 45n29, 48n37, 59-60, 61, 77-78, 103-104, 106n10, 107-108
Frein, B., 1n2
Funk, R. W., xvi, 7-8, 14, 16n12, 18n19-20, 23n43, 39n1, 48n37

Garrett, S. R., 8, 42, 81nn15-16, 85n29, 93-94, 96-97, 98n88, 99n92, 100
Gaventa, B. R., 6, 22, 52nn53-54, 54, 81n18
Genette, G., 14n2, 16n12
Goulder, M. D., 8, 41, 42n10, 58nn81-82
Green, J. B., 3
Grumm, M. H., 21n31

Habel, N. C., 87
Haenchen, E., 18, 22, 26, 41, 52, 53n57, 55n68, 75, 82n22, 83n25, 90n54, 92, 94n69, 95n71, 96n76
Hamm, M. D., 8n42, 30n73, 47n35, 52-53, 54n62, 69

Index of Modern Authors

Harvey, J. D., 1n3
Hemer, C. J., 58n85
Hilgert, E., 57n79
Hooker, M., 6
House, P. R., 4, 35

Iser, W., 20n29

Johnson, L. T., 62, 67, 81n14, 89–90

Käsemann, E., 3
Keathley, N. H., xvi
Keel, O., 42, 43n18, 57n74, 66n26, 70n44
Kilgallen, J. J., 26n55, 34
Kim, H. M., 1n2
Kingsbury, J. D., 81n13
Krašovec, J., 80, 80n4
Kurz, W. S., 14, 30n73

Lasine, S., 81n6
Lowth, R., 80n3

MacLennan, R. S., 110n16
Maddox, R., 21n32, 25
Marguerat, D., 92n58
Marshall, I. H., 3, 52, 53n56, 92n60
Martin, R., 42n14
Mittelstadt, M., 5
Moessner, D. P., xvi, 4, 9n43, 23–25, 29–31, 33–35, 37, 49n40, 50n43, 99n89
Moule, C. F. D., 50n46
Munck, J., 93n63

Nestle, W., 88n44
Neyrey, J., 50n45

O'Toole, R. F., 9nn42–43, 30–31, 69n38, 83n24
Owen, H. P., 50n47

Parsons, M. C., xiii, xvi, 11, 17n17, 47n35, 53, 71, 89n45, 90
Patterson, S. J., 5n26,
Pervo, R. I., xvi, 8, 11, 41, 42n10, 56n72, 57n74, 58n81, 85n32, 108n15
Pilch, J. J., 64n14, 68, 70n42, 73n54,

Polhill, J., 4, 13n1, 18n21, 24n48, 68, 70n45, 76, 82n21, 89, 92nn59–60, 93n63, 94n69
Porter, R. J., 24
Powell, M. A., 10n44, 40n4
Praeder, S. M., 40n3, 56n71, 58–59, 62
Prinsloo, W. S., 81n10

Rackham, R., 8, 41, 42n10, 52–54, 58nn81–82
Radl, W., 8, 57n80, 58n81
Reeves, R., 42
Reicke, B., 22
Rhoads, D. M., 2n7
Richard, E., 49n40, 98n86
Rimmon-Kenan, S., 14n2, 15n8, 16, 27
Rowe, C. K., 28

Samain, P., 94n67
Sandmel, S., 40n3
Scroggs, R., 54n67
Schütz, F., 4n19
Sheeley, S. M., 15, 23n43, 27
Stagg, F., 65n17, 94n69
Sternberg, M., 16

Talbert, C. H., 5n27, 9n43, 49, 52n52, 56n73, 62
Tannehill, R. C., xvi, 4, 10n45, 14n7, 15, 17, 18n21, 19nn24–25, 21, 22n33, 24n46, 24n48, 27, 28n64, 39n2, 40n5, 41, 49n40, 50n43, 51n50, 55, 63n10, 65–67, 70n44, 72, 74n58, 99n90, 106n8
Terrell, J. M., 5n27
Thompson, D. A., 5n27
Trémel, B., 9n42, 65–67
Trocmé, É., 49n40
Tuckett, C. M., 28
Tyson, J. B., 3, 14n7, 17n17, 111n17

Uspensky, B., 28n64

Viviano, B. T., 42n12

Walworth, A., 15

Weaver, J. D., 5n27
Weiser, A., 80n5
Westermann, C., 80n3
Williams, D., 76, 85, 94n69

Zeller, E., 49

Index of Scripture and Ancient Writings

OLD TESTAMENT

Genesis

39:21–23	105n6
40:14	105n6

Deuteronomy

13:1–5	99
18:9–14	99n89
18:15	99n89
18:18	99n89
18:20	99
28:25–26	100n93
28:28–29	98
28:39	87n40
29:17	96n74
29:18	96
29:20	96
30:12–13	57n78
30:18	96
31:16	43n20

Leviticus

24:23	70

Joshua

7:1	92
7:2–5	92n59
7:20–21	92

Judges

3:12–25	91n56
3:22–23	91n56
3:24	91n56
4:21	93

1 Kings

1:21	43n20
2:10	43n20
11:21	43n20
15:8	43n20
17:22	64n14
17:23	64n16
18	99
18:40	99
21:13	70n46

2 Kings

4:18–37	65
4:35	64n14
8:24	43n20
9:32–33	90
13:9	43n20
19:35	86
23:6	55n70, 70n46

1 Samuel

25:38	86

2 Samuel

7:12	43n20
20:10	91
22	57

2 Chronicles

9:31	43n20
13:12	86
13:15	86
13:20	86
23:14–15	70n46
26:23	43n20

Job

2:9	88n41
3:16	98
7:5	88n41
17:13	43n17
17:14	87
21:26	87
38	57
38:17	46n30

Psalms

1	80–81, 110
13:3	43n20
16:8–11	82n21
18	57
22:29	67n26
23:4	43n17
28:1	67n26
49:14	43n17
49:19	42
58:8b	43n16
63:9	67n26
68	57
68:20	57
68:22	57
69	57, 88n43
88:6	43n17
88:11	67n26
107	57
107:10	42
107:16	46n30
107:18	46n30
107:23–32	57n74
109	88n43
115:18	71
118:22	31

Proverbs

7:27	43n17
10:5	80n5
12:4	87n40
25:20	87n40

Isaiah

14	86n35, 90n55
14:4–20	100
14:11	100
14:15	100n96
14:19	100n96
14:21–23	100
53:7–8	23
58:6	96n75
59:9–10	53

Jeremiah

26:23	55n70
28:16	99
28:17	99
29:21–23	99n91
35:16 LXX	99
35:17 LXX	99
36:21–23 LXX	99n91
51:57	43n20

Ezekiel

21:7	93
26	57
27–28	86n35

Habakkuk

1:5	83

NEW TESTAMENT

Matthew

6:19–20	84n26
7:13–14	81n12
8:12	43
22:13	43, 44
25:30	43
26:37–45	66n24
27:63–66	44n24

Mark

9:47–48	87n37
14:34–41	66n24
15:33	43

Luke

2:25–35	72n50
2:36–38	72n50
4:5–7	100
4:6–7	100n94
4:18	96
5:11	90
5:22	95
7:11–17	11n48
7:12	55n70, 70
7:12–15	72n50
7:14	76n62
7:15	64n14
8:41–56	11n48, 65, 72n50
8:50	67n28
8:52	65
8:54	73, 76n62
8:55	64nn13–14, 73n53
9:7	46n31
9:9	41
9:22	56
9:44	41n8
10:18	100, 100n94
12:8	50n46
17:25	56
18:32	41n8
19:39	55
19:47	55
19:48	55
20:1	55
20:19	41, 55
20:35–38	51n49
22:1	41, 67
22:1—24:53	11n48
22:2	41, 55
22:3	89n45
22:3–6	95
22:4	55
22:7	41
22:12	67
22:15	16n13
22:31–32	89n45
22:45	66n24
22:45–46	66
22:46	66n24
22:52	47
22:53	41n7
22:54	41
22:63	47
22:66	47n33, 49
22:66–67	49
22:69	49, 50, 50n44
22:71	49
23:2	49
23:13	41
23:25	41n8
23:32	41
23:33	44n23
23:34	49
23:44	43
23:44–45	54, 57
23:46	49
23:53	64, 70
23:55	70
24:1	67

Index of Scripture and Ancient Writings   131

24:3–4	46
24:4	44n25
24:5	55
24:5–6	46
24:7	41n8, 56
24:9	46n32, 47
24:10	45
24:11	45
24:15–31	45
24:20	41n8
24:22	55
24:25	33
24:26	16n13, 30n72, 56
24:27–34	33
24:30–35	67
24:32	19
24:33–35	47
24:36–43	54
24:36–49	17
24:36–51	45
24:37	45n27, 55, 71
24:41	64n14, 71
24:41–43	73n53
24:44–51	56
24:45–46	19
24:46	16n13, 17, 19, 30, 45, 54
24:47–49	45
24:51	45

John

8:12	81n11
9:1–41	81n11
9:39–41	81n11
11:11	65n18
11:11–14	43
11:13	65n18
11:44	44
19:20	70n46
19:40	44

Acts

1:1–3	15
1:3	16–17, 21, 22n39, 26n57, 56, 64, 67, 71, 105
1:8	26n57, 78, 105
1:13	67
1:16	88–89
1:16–20	88–91
1:17	95
1:18	89, 90n52
1:20	88
1:21–22	26n57
1:22	26n57
2	28
2:14–36	105
2:14–40	28–29
2:22	29
2:22–36	65
2:23	28
2:23–24	28, 82
2:24	96
2:25–36	82–83
2:27	82
2:28	82
2:29	82
2:31	82
2:32	26n57
2:32–33	29
2:34	82
2:36	29
2:41	65
3:1–4:22	48
3:1–4:31	47n35, 69–71, 106
3:2	69–71, 73
3:4	73
3:6	69n37, 72
3:7	69, 71
3:7–8	71
3:8	73
3:8–9	71
3:9	71
3:10–11	71
3:11–26	26, 29–31, 48, 48n38

Acts (continued)

3:12–15	72	5:17–41	45–46, 49, 62n5, 105
3:13	29	5:18	45
3:14–15	30	5:19	46
3:15	69, 69n37	5:20	46, 70n44
3:15–16	48	5:21	46
3:17–18	30	5:22–23	46
3:18	16n13, 30	5:24	46
3:21–22	30	5:25	46
3:22	30, 69n38	5:29–32	32
3:24	30	5:30	46, 69n37
3:26	30, 69n38	5:30–31	50n45
3:38	54n67	5:31	32
4:1	47	5:36	94, 94n68
4:1–2	25	5:39	86, 109
4:1–3	73	5:41	109
4:1–21	46–49, 105	5:42	20, 22n36
4:1–23	62n5	6:11	49
4:2	25, 47, 47n33	6:12	49
4:3	47	6:13	49
4:3–21	49	7:1	49
4:5	47	7:37	35
4:8–12	26, 31, 48	7:52	35
4:10	31, 48, 69, 69n37	7:54	49
4:11	31	7:54–60	106
4:14	48	7:55	50
4:21	47, 71	7:55–56	49
4:21–22	48	7:57–59	49
4:22	48, 71	7:59	49–51
4:23	47	7:60	43, 49, 66
4:25–28	88n44	8:1	19n23
4:25–29	109	8:2	50
4:31	92	8:3	19n23
4:32	92	8:4	21, 94, 95n72
4:32ff	89	8:5	21
4:33	25–26	8:9	94
5:1–11	67n29, 91–93	8:9–24	94–96
5:2	92	8:12	21, 22n35
5:3	92	8:13	94
5:5	75, 92	8:14	94
5:6	93	8:18–19	95
5:9	92	8:20	95
5:10	92–93	8:20–21	96
5:12	92	8:21	95
		8:23	95–96

8:24	96	10:26	69n37, 75
8:25	22n35	10:34–43	32
8:32–33	23–24	10:38–42	32
8:32–35	21	10:39–40	76
8:33	23	10:39–43	26, 26n57
8:35	20	10:40	69n37, 76n61
8:36	23	10:40–41	26n57
8:36–39	54n67	10:41	76
8:38	24	10:43	32, 76
8:40	20n28, 22n36	10:47–48	54n67
9	52	10:48	76
9:1–19	51–52, 106	11:19–20	21
9:4	77	11:20	22n35
9:4–5	85n31	12	8
9:5	59	12:1–19	41–45, 105
9:8	53, 69n37, 98n88	12:2	41
9:8–9	53	12:3	41, 85
9:11	98n88	12:4	41, 85
9:15	55	12:6	42–44
9:16	56, 108	12:6–7	66
9:18–19	54	12:7	44, 69n37, 86
9:19	54	12:12–17	45
9:19–20	18n20, 55	12:14	45
9:20	22nn35–36	12:15	45, 45n27
9:20–22	32	12:17	45
9:21	55	12:19	85, 85n30
9:26	55	12:20–23	85–88
9:31–43	62	12:23	67n29, 86, 92
9:32–35	72–73	13:2	97
9:34	72–73	13:5	22n35, 97
9:35	33n79, 73	13:6	97
9:36	63	13:6–11	97–100
9:36–42	63–65	13:8	97
9:36–43	65	13:9	97
9:37	70n43	13:10	97, 97n85
9:39	63	13:11	97–98, 100
9:40	64, 73–74, 76n62	13:16–41	32–34, 83–84, 106
9:41	64, 67	13:22	34, 83
9:42	65, 73	13:23	32, 34
10	106	13:26	34
10:1–48	74–77	13:27–39	32
10:11	75	13:28–29	33
10:24–48	111	13:29	33
10:25	75	13:30	69n37, 83

Acts (continued)

13:32	34	18:24	21
13:33	33–34	18:28	20–21
13:34	83	19:2–6	54n67
13:35	83	19:8	21–22, 22n39
13:36	43, 83, 93	20:6	67
13:37	69n37, 83	20:6–12	106
13:38	33, 83	20:7	66
13:38–39	34	20:7–12	65–68
13:41	83	20:9	66
13:46	83	20:9–12	65
13:46–47	83, 83n23	20:10	65, 67
13:47–48	83	20:12	67
14:1	55	20:25	21–22, 22n39
14:1–20	51, 55–56, 106	20:28–31	66
14:2	55	21:27	52
14:4	55	22:1–16	52
14:5	55	22:11	98n88
14:7	20n28, 22n36, 74	23:6	27n59, 47n33
14:8	73	23:6–10	37
14:8–11	73–74	23:11	26n57
14:9	73	24:10–21	37
14:10	73–74	24:14	37
14:11	55	24:15	27n59
14:19	25, 55, 73	24:21	27n59, 37
14:20	56, 111	25:14–21	34–35
14:21	20n28, 22n36	25:15	34
14:21–24	56	25:19	35
14:22	24–25, 56, 108	26:1–23	35
16:6–7	76	26:6–7	35
16:10	20n28	26:8	35, 69n37
16:33	54n67	26:13	98n88
17:2–4	15, 17–19	26:18	53n61, 95
17:2–3	18, 18n21, 21, 22n36	26:22–23	35
17:3	16n13, 18, 20, 22n35, 27, 30, 30n72, 38	26:23	16n13, 30, 30n72
17:5–9	18	26:27	35
17:13	22n35	27	8
17:18	25, 27	27:1–44	51, 106
17:22–31	36	27:4–44	62n5
17:23	36	27:14–44	56–59
17:30	36	27:20	57
17:31	36	27:39	57
18:4–5	21	27:44	57
18:5	20, 22n35, 26n57	28:23	21, 22n35, 22n39
		28:31	21, 22n35, 105

Index of Scripture and Ancient Writings   135

Romans	
5:14–21	81n9
6:3–11	54n67
10:7	44n22

1 Corinthians	
15:18	43
15:50–52	43

2 Corinthians	
1:9–10	42

Philippians	
2:5–11	81n10
3:10	42

Hebrews	
13:12	71n46

Revelation	
13	86n35
17	86n35
20:1–3	44
20:13	57n79
20:14–15	57n79

DEUTEROCANONICAL AND PSEUDEPIGRAPHAL WRITINGS

Judith	
16:17	86

Life of Adam and Eve	
12:1—16:3	100n95

2 Maccabees	
9:5	86n33
9:7–28	90n52
9:8	90n52
9:9	87, 87n41

Sirach (Wisdom of Ben Sira)	
10:11	87
19:3	87

ANCIENT AUTHORS

Apollonius of Rhodes

Argonautica	
2.609–10	57n76

Herodotus

Persian Wars	
4:205	87n37

Josephus

Antiquities of the Jews	
16:99	98n87
17:169	87n38
18:59	90n55
20:97	94n68

Wars of the Jews	
1:621	90n55
6:64	90n53
7:453	91n57

Lucian of Samosata

Alexander the False Prophet
59   87n37

Pausanius

Description of Greece
9.7.2–3   87n37

Philostratus

Life of Appolonius
1:317   10n47

Pliny the Elder

Natural History
7:172   87n37

Posidonius

Fragment 5
57   90n55

Xenophon

Ephesian Tale
1–5   10n47

www.ingramcontent.com/pod-product-compliance
Lightning Source LLC
Chambersburg PA
CBHW072146160426
43197CB00012B/2271